DK EYEWITNESS

T0047082

TOP10
BANGKOK

Top 10 Bangkok Highlights

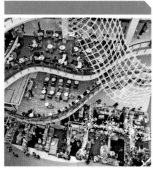

The Top 10 of Everything

CONTENTS

Bangkok Area by Area

Streetsmart

Within each Top 10 list in this book, no hierarchy of quality or popularity is implied. All 10 are, in the editor's opinion, of roughly equal merit.

Throughout this book, floors are referred to in accordance with American usage; i.e., the "first floor" is at ground level.

Title page, front cover and spine *The stunning Wat Benjamabophit at sunrise*
Back cover, clockwise from top left
Wat Arun; Bangkok cityscape; Chinatown; Wat Benjamabophit; Damnoen Saduak Floating Market

The rapid rate at which the world is changing is constantly keeping the DK Eyewitness team on our toes. While we've worked hard to ensure that this edition of Bangkok is accurate and up-to-date, we know that opening hours alter, standards shift, prices fluctuate, places close and new ones pop up in their stead. So, if you notice we've got something wrong or left something out, we want to hear about it. Please get in touch at **travelguides@dk.com**

Welcome to
Bangkok

A study in contrasts, Bangkok is simultaneously traditional and modern, noisy and serene. Outside even the glitziest Western-style building, you'll find a small but well-tended shrine respecting the spirit of the land. A city of surprises, it's held together by the famed hospitality of the Thai people. With DK Eyewitness Top 10 Bangkok, it's yours to explore.

The massive **Chao Phraya River** bisects Bangkok as it flows into the nearby Gulf of Thailand. Along its eastern bank lies the **Old City**, centered around **Rattanakosin**, Bangkok's royal heart, with its spectacular **Grand Palace**, the gleaming treasures of the **National Museum**, and a number of Buddhist temples.

Just downstream lie **Chinatown**'s markets, gold shops, and Taoist shrines. Bangkokians have embraced their riverside roots, and many art galleries and hip pubs take advantage of the lowrise buildings on the river and cool breezes. Inland, you'll find ultramodern downtown hotels, restaurants, and shops, especially among the glass skyscrapers in Silom. Across the river, in **Thonburi**, the unique Khmer-style temple of **Wat Arun** and quiet canals offer a glimpse of a life that could not be more different from the one just over the water.

Whether you're visiting for a weekend or a week, our Top 10 guide brings together the best of everything the city has to offer, from the temples and museums of the Old City to the nightlife of Downtown. The guide has useful tips throughout, from seeking out what's free to getting off the beaten path, plus seven easy-to-follow itineraries, designed to tie together a clutch of sights in a short space of time. Add inspiring photography and detailed maps, and you've got the essential pocket-sized travel companion. **Enjoy the book, and enjoy Bangkok**.

Clockwise from top: **Giant feet of a Buddha image at Wat Indrawiharn**, a boat filled with hats in Damnoen Saduak Floating Market, traffic on Yaowarat Road in Chinatown, lakeside pavilion at Muang Boran, Buddha statues at Wat Pho, the Emerald Green Pagoda at Wat Pak Nam, near Khlong Bangkok Yai, a cannonball flower

Exploring Bangkok

Although Bangkok is huge, many of its sights are within walking distance of each other along the river or in nearby Downtown. Using a combination of river boats and mass transit, it's largely possible to avoid the notorious traffic jams. Here are our suggestions for the best things to experience in either two or four days.

Rattanakosin art from the 18th to 20th centuries can be admired in the National Museum.

Wat Phra Kaeo is a complex of prayer halls, towers, and *chedis* (stupas) within the grounds of the Grand Palace.

National Museum
Brown Suga
The Jazz
Boutique
Royal Barge
Museum
Tha Maharaj
Queen Sirikit
Museum
of Textiles
Wat Phra Kaeo
Grand Palace
from Ayutthaya
50 miles (80 km)
Wat Arun
Wat Pho

0 kilometers 1
0 miles 1

Two Days in Bangkok

Day ❶
MORNING
Start off with a visit to the magnificent **Wat Phra Kaeo** (see pp12–13) and the adjacent **Grand Palace** (see pp14–15), taking time for the excellent Queen Sirikit Museum of Textiles. Walk down to the Chao Phraya River and have lunch at one of the small restaurants at **Tha Maharaj** (see p73).

AFTERNOON
After lunch, stroll the grounds of **Wat Pho** (see pp18–19) and enjoy a back rub in the temple's massage school. Next, visit the **National Museum** (see pp16–17). Have dinner at the **Blue Elephant** restaurant (see p99), then board the boat from Tha Saphan Taksin to Asiatique the Riverfront and take in the **Calypso Cabaret** (see p101).

Day ❷
MORNING
Take a water taxi to **Wat Arun** (see pp30–31), then hop on the Saen Saeb canal boat to **Jim Thompson House** (see pp28–9), the home of the American who helped revive the Thai silk industry.

AFTERNOON
Browse the **shopping malls** (see p89) on Rama I Road, then head to the **Muangthai Rachadalai Theatre** for a traditional dance show (see p101).

Asiatique The Riverfront, Calypso Cabare

Four Days in Bangkok

Day ❶
MORNING
Cross the river to Thonburi to visit the stunning "Temple of Dawn",

Damnoen Saduak Floating Market is renowned for its noodle sellers, who prepare delicious traditional dishes inside *sampan* (rowing boats) on the canal.

Beyond Bangkok

0 km   40
0 miles   40

Ayutthaya

see area of main map

Damnoen Saduak Floating Market

Bight of Bangkok

bicycle or hire a tuk-tuk to visit the many temples and museums.

AFTERNOON

Indulge yourself with a treatment at one of Bangkok's many excellent spas *(see pp46–7)*, then take in the sunset from **Tha Maharaj** *(see p73)*.

Day ❸
MORNING

Wake early to visit the **Damnoen Saduak Floating Market** *(see pp24–5)*.

AFTERNOON

Enjoy the contemporary artworks on display at **Number 1 Gallery** on Silom 21 *(19 Soi Silom 21)*.

Day ❹
MORNING

Head to **Wat Pho** *(see pp18–19)*, admire the huge **Reclining Buddha**, and spare some time afterwards for a traditional massage on the temple grounds.

AFTERNOON

Visit **Jim Thompson House** *(see pp28–9)*, followed by a shopping trip to nearby **Siam Paragon** *(see p89)* and the other malls on Rama I Road.

Jim Thompson House

Siam Paragon

Rama I Road

Muangthai Rachadalai Theatre
4 miles (6 km)

BOAT

from Damnoen Saduak Floating Market
50 miles (80 km)

Silom Road

Saphan Taksin

Number 1 Gallery

Blue Elephant

Key

— Two-day itinerary
— Four-day itinerary

Wat Arun *(see pp30–31)*, and the **Royal Barge Museum** *(see p96)*.

AFTERNOON

Visit the **Wat Phra Kaeo** *(see pp12–13)*, **Grand Palace** *(see pp14–15)*, and the **National Museum** *(see pp16–17)*. Dine on the river *(see p90)*, then listen to some jazz at **Brown Sugar: The Jazz Boutique** *(see p74)*.

Day ❷
MORNING

Visit the ancient Siamese capital of **Ayutthaya** *(see pp32–5)*. Rent a

Jim Thompson House, a delightful treasure trove of the most exquisite Southeast Asian antiques and art.

Top 10 Bangkok Highlights

**Buddha statues under a colonnade
at the temple of Wat Arun**

Bangkok Highlights

Spiritual and sensual, Bangkok is one of Asia's most intriguing cities. Its glittering temples and museums overflow with art, while the city's canals and markets bustle with local life. Shopping, dining out, and reveling in the vibrant nightlife should feature high on everyone's itinerary.

Wat Phra Kaeo ①
A fabulous patchwork of colors and shapes, the Wat Phra Kaeo temple is Thailand's holiest site, and is the pinnacle of perfection in Thai religious art and architecture *(see pp12–13)*.

② Grand Palace
A dazzling complex comprising a number of historic buildings, pavilions, courtyards and gardens. An unmissable sight *(see pp14–15)*.

③ National Museum
One of the largest museums in Asia, it has priceless exhibits including intricate works of art that document the long and eventful history of Thailand *(see pp16–17)*.

Wat Pho ④
Bangkok's oldest and biggest temple, and formerly a center for public education, Wat Pho houses a massive Reclining Buddha and a school of Thai massage *(see pp18–19)*.

Bangkok's Canals ⑤
Boats were once the city's main mode of transport. Tour the canals to glimpse a vanishing lifestyle *(see pp20–21)*.

6 Damnoen Saduak Floating Market

Though designed for tourists, the colorful sights, aromatic smells, and cheerful banter of vendors make a visit to this floating market a delightful experience (see pp24–5).

7 Chatuchak Weekend Market

Bangkok's biggest market offers the chance to pick up a unique souvenir and feel the pulse of Thai culture in the maze of stalls (see pp26–7).

8 Jim Thompson House

This complex is a fine example of Thai teak architecture. The main house remains as it was in the days of Jim Thompson, the man who helped make Thai silk famous (see pp28–9).

9 Wat Arun

With its five distinctive *prangs* (towers), which are often used as a logo of the city, this temple played an important historical role in the development of Bangkok and remains one of its most attractive sights (see pp30–31).

10 Ayutthaya

The ancient city of Ayutthaya is easily visited in a day. Its huge, crumbling *chedis* (stupas) and blissful Buddha images give an idea of the splendor of this former capital (see pp32–5).

★ Wat Phra Kaeo

The spectacular Wat Phra Kaeo is Thailand's holiest temple, and lies inside of the Grand Palace complex. It serves as home to the national talisman, the Emerald Buddha, and as the royal chapel of the Grand Palace. There are no resident monks here, and the lavish assemblage is kept in pristine condition. Heavily ornamented statues of mythical creatures called *yakshas* (giants), from Thai legends, stand at the entrance gates, acting as guardians of the temple. It is a stunning display of Thailand's artistic and architectural finesse, and a truly memorable sight.

1 Ramakien Murals
Stretching over half a mile (1 km) along the temple's cloister walls, the *Ramakien* murals **(above)** portray scenes from the Hindu epic *Ramayana* in 178 panels of intricate detail and vibrant color.

2 Phra Mondop
This repository for sacred Buddhist texts is on the upper terrace. Its deep-green mosaics are a perfect backdrop for the seated stone Buddhas in each corner.

3 Phra Si Rattana Chedi
This glittering *chedi* (stupa) is shaped like a cone, and stands majestically on the upper terrace beside the Phra Mondop. It is built of gold tiles in the Sri Lankan style.

5 Model of Angkor Wat
Tucked away behind the Phra Mondop, this scale model of Angkor Wat was commissioned by Rama IV (see p38), when Cambodia was under Siamese rule.

4 Royal Pantheon
The pantheon **(left)**, one of a trio of tall buildings on the upper terrace, dates back to the reign of Rama IV. It enshrines life-sized statues of the past rulers of the Chakri dynasty (see p38).

6 Wihan Yot
Also known as "the porcelain *wihan*", this delicately adorned prayer hall stands to the north of Phra Mondop. It contains a number of Buddha images, including the Nak buddha rescued from Ayutthaya.

7 The Emerald Buddha

Carved out of single piece of jadeite rather than emerald, the most sacred image **(left)** in the kingdom is just 26 in (66 cm) tall. Thought to have been crafted in Sri Lanka, it was housed in Chiang Rai, Lampang, and Laos before Rama I brought it to Bangkok.

MYTHICAL CREATURES IN THAI TEMPLES

A panoply of fearsome creatures guard the entrances to most Thai temple compounds. These are from the legendary forest of Himaphan, a kind of Buddhist Shangri-La up in the Himalayan Mountains. These include *singha*, a lion-like figure, *yaksha*, a giant, *naga*, a serpent-like protector of Buddha, *hongsa*, a swan-like entity, and several other hybrids that are part-man and part-beast.

8 The Bot

The most visited building in the grounds is the *bot* (ordination hall), which contains the much-venerated Emerald Buddha. Inside, the walls are adorned with murals, and the scent of incense is over-whelming as Thais pay respect to the image that is revered as the country's talisman.

Temple of the Jewel containing Lord Buddha

NEED TO KNOW

MAP B4 ■ Na Phra Lan Road ■ Chao Phraya express boat to Tha Chang ■ www.royalgrandpalace. th/en

Open 8:30am–3:30pm daily

Adm B500, including Grand Palace (see pp14-15)

■ Dress modestly. Before entering the premises, make sure you are not wearing sandals, shorts, short skirts, torn or tight trousers, or sleeveless or see-through shirts.

■ The ticket office is outside the western wall of Wat Phra Kaeo, near the temple's entrance.

9 Hor Phra Nak and Hor Phra Monthien Tham

Flanking the Wihan Yot are the Hor Phra Nak, a royal mausoleum with urns that hold the ashes of members of the royal family, and the Hor Phra Monthien Tham, a library that has particularly fine doors inlaid with mother-of-pearl.

10 Chapel of Gandahara Buddha

In the southeast corner of the temple compound stands a small chapel with beautifully painted doors. Usually locked, it contains an image, used in the Royal Ploughing Ceremony (see p64), of the Buddha calling down the rains.

⭐ Grand Palace

In 1782, King Rama I (r.1782–1809) established Bangkok as Siam's capital and built Wat Phra Kaeo to house the most precious Buddha image in the country. In 1784, he had the adjacent Grand Palace complex built, which became the home of the royal family. Its structure was significantly enhanced by later rulers. No king has resided here since the early 20th century, but the palace's several buildings, ceremonial halls, pavilions, and gardens display a fantastic fusion of Thai and Western aesthetic.

1 Dusit Throne Hall

For many, this building **(left)** is the site's crowning glory, featuring a four-tiered roof and Rama I's teak throne.

2 Amarin Winichai Hall

This building was originally used as an audience hall for foreign guests. Inside, the hall has colorful murals and Rama I's boat-shaped Busabok Mala Throne surmounted by a nine-tiered white canopy. Today, the hall is used for state ceremonies and is open to the public on weekdays.

3 Inner Palace

Until the time of Rama VII (r.1925–35), the Inner Palace was inhabited solely by women. All males except the king were forbidden entry. Still closed to the public, it is now a school for girls from prominent families.

4 Chakri Maha Prasat

Occupying center stage in the Grand Palace is the Chakri throne hall **(below)**. Built in 1882 by Rama V (r.1868–1910), it fuses Western and Thai architecture. The ashes of Chakri kings are housed here.

NEED TO KNOW

MAP B4 ■ Na Phra Lan Road ■ Chao Phraya express boat to Tha Chang ■ www.royal grandpalace.th/en

Open 8:30am–3:30pm daily

Adm B500, including Wat Phra Kaeo (see pp12–13) and the Queen Sirikit Museum of Textiles

Queen Sirikit Museum of Textiles: 9am–4:30pm daily (last entry 3:30pm); adm B150 (museum only)

■ Dress modestly; no sandals, shorts, short skirts, torn or tight trousers, sleeveless shirts, crop tops or see-through tops.

■ Carry water, as the only café is at the end of the tour, next to the Dusit Throne Hall.

5 Model of Mount Krailas

Behind the Dusit Throne Hall is an ornamented model of Mount Krailas, thought to be the central mountain of the universe in Hindu and Buddhist mythology. In olden times, royal children would have their topknot cut off here, in an elaborate ceremony to welcome adolescence.

7 Aphonphimok Pavilion

This small but attractive wooden pavilion **(right)** was built by Rama IV (r.1851–68) as a royal changing room prior to giving audiences in the adjacent Dusit Throne Hall. Its multi-tiered roof and gold decoration are hallmarks of traditional Thai architecture.

9 Wat Phra Kaeo Museum

This museum (see p13) displays a treasure trove of artifacts salvaged from restoration of the palace, such as former costumes of the Emerald Buddha.

10 Queen Sirikit Museum of Textiles

Formerly the site of the Royal Treasury, this building, constructed from white Italian marble, now houses a textile museum. On display is ceremonial and modern royal attire, with an emphasis on Thai silk garments, plus pieces from elsewhere in Asia.

Panoramic view of the Grand Palace at night

6 Phaisan Thaksin Hall

This hall is not open to the public and is used only for coronations. It contains the Coronation Chair and the tutelary deity, Phra Siam Thewathirat.

Map of the Grand Palace

8 Siwalai Gardens

These well-manicured, picturesque gardens were once used for official receptions. Located within the gardens are the Phra Buddha Ratana Sathan, built as a personal chapel by Rama IV (see p38), and Boromphiman Mansion, built in the Neo-Classical style by Rama V (see p38) for the Crown Prince. It is now used as a guesthouse for visiting dignitaries.

ENTERING AND GETTING AROUND THE COMPLEX

Entry is via the gate on Na Phra Lan Road, where anyone inappropriately dressed is required to borrow clothes. The ticket office is outside the western wall of Wat Phra Kaeo (see pp12–13), near the temple's entrance. Visitors usually walk clockwise around Wat Phra Kaeo before exiting the temple through its southern wall and exploring the rest of the Grand Palace. Allow about two hours to walk around the site.

🔟⭐ National Museum

Thailand's premier museum offers a great introduction to Thai history. Inside, the Buddhaisawan Chapel is one of the country's most precious treasures, as is the Phra Sihing Buddha image it houses. Other highlights include well-preserved fragments of Dvaravati and Srivijaya statues, and the royal funeral chariots.

4 Lanna Art
Several small Buddha images from northern Thailand in the Lanna period (13th to 16th centuries) are on display here.

5 Phra Sihing Buddha Image
One of three such images claiming to be the original, this small but superbly crafted Sukhothai-style sculpture sits on a pedestal in the Buddhaisawan Chapel and is bathed in a golden glow.

1 Buddhaisawan Chapel
This beautiful chapel **(above)**, built in 1787 for the Second King, now sits at the heart of the National Museum complex. Its rich murals, polished floors, gilt Buddha images, and hushed atmosphere make it a star sight.

3 Rattanakosin Art
A gallery in the north wing displays art and furnishings from the 18th- to 20th century Rattanakosin era **(right)**. These pieces combine traditional and Western elements.

6 Red House
A fine example of an Ayutthaya-style teak house, the Red House was originally the home of Rama I's older sister, Sri Sudarak. It has a multitiered roof decorated with beautiful carvings, and the interior contains some antique royal furnishings.

2 Ayutthayan Art
Huge, serene Buddha heads, as well as scripture cabinets adorned with scenes of Ayutthaya in its heyday *(see pp32–3)*, are displayed in the Ayutthayan gallery.

7 Thailand's Past
Located in the former Sivamokhaphiman Throne Hall, this gallery contains over a hundred superbly displayed and lighted examples of the finest antiquities and treasures from Thailand.

NEED TO KNOW

MAP B3 ■ Na Phra That Road ■ 02 224 1333 ■ Chao Phraya express boat to Tha Chang ■ www.finearts.go.th/museumbangkok

Open 9am–4pm Wed–Sun

Adm B200

■ Join the free guided tours in English, French, German, and Japanese at 9:30am on Wednesdays and Thursdays.

■ The museum covers a big area, but there are seats in shaded corners between galleries where you can take a break.

■ There is a café right at the museum entrance where you can buy snacks, ice creams, and cold drinks.

8 Sukhothai Art

Sukhothai art (dating from the mid-13th century to the mid-15th century) is often described as the apex of Thai artistic skill. The flowing lines of walking and sitting Buddha images **(right)** inside the museum bear testament to this idea.

9 Royal Funeral Chariots Gallery

The elaborately decorated carriages in this gallery give an idea of the pomp and ceremony that accompany royal funerals. Each of the gilded teak carriages weighs several tons and needs hundreds of men to pull it.

ORIGIN OF THE NATIONAL MUSEUM

The National Museum was originally the Wang Na (Palace of the Front), built in 1782 by Rama I for his younger brother and deputy. However, in 1887, Rama V decided to turn the building into a public museum so that his subjects could appreciate their rich cultural heritage.

Floorplan of National Museum

Key to Floorplan
- First floor
- Second floor

- Dvaravati Wheel of Law **10**
- **2** Ayutthayan Art
- Lanna Art **4**
- Phra Sihing Buddha Image **5**
- Red House **6**
- Thailand's Past **7**
- **8** Sukhothai Art
- **3** Rattanakosin Art
- Buddhaisawan Chapel **1**
- **9** Royal Funeral Chariots Gallery

10 Dvaravati Wheel of Law

Dvaravati art flourished from the 6th to the 9th centuries, and this 8th-century stone wheel **(left)** set above a deer is a great example. Located on the second floor of the south wing, it represents the Buddha's first sermon in Sarnath, India.

TOP 10 ⭐ Wat Pho

Bangkok's oldest and largest temple, Wat Pho contains the awe-inspiring Reclining Buddha. Built in the 16th century and reconstructed by Rama I, it is a typical Thai temple, with resident monks, a school, massage pavilions, and a strong community spirit. Around the grounds are a large number of statues and *chedis* (stupas) glittering with mosaics.

3 Feet of the Reclining Buddha

The soles of the feet of the Reclining Buddha are inlaid with 108 *lakshanas*, or auspicious characteristics that identify the true Buddha. Crafted in shimmering mother-of-pearl, these images are a dazzling work of art.

1 Reclining Buddha

The huge Reclining Buddha **(above)**, made of brick, plaster, and gold leaf, fills the *wihan* (assembly hall) in the northwest corner of the compound. Admire its serene expression and its feet, studded with mother-of-pearl inlay.

2 Traditional Massage

Wat Pho is known as a center for traditional medicine and since the 1960s has run what is considered the best massage school in Thailand. Highly trained masseurs are on hand to relieve visitors of their aches and pains. The school also offers 5-day massage courses.

Map of Wat Pho

4 Miniature Mountains

On several man-made mounds around the complex are statues of hermits in unusual postures. These are intended to teach people about the healing positions for the body.

5 Medicine Pavilion

In the heart of the complex, the Medicine Pavilion has stone tablets **(left)** indicating the pressure points on the body used during traditional Thai massage.

NEED TO KNOW

MAP B5 ▪ Soi Chetuphon ▪ 02 226 0335 ▪ Chao Phraya express boat to Tha Tien ▪ www.watpho.com

Open 8am–6:30pm daily

Adm B200

▪ Most visitors enter from Thanon Thai Wang, next to the Reclining Buddha. However, the southern entrance on Soi Chetuphon allows you to appreciate the rest of the compound in comparative peace before finally arriving at the temple's most popular highlight.

▪ Several small food shops line the western border of the temple.

RECLINING BUDDHAS

A Reclining Buddha appears to be relaxing or even sleeping, but this interpretation could not be farther from the truth. While other images of Buddha standing, sitting, or walking show aspects of his quest to attain Enlightenment, a Reclining Buddha symbolizes his arrival at Nirvana, a state of true all-knowing awareness that is the complete antithesis of relaxation or sleep.

9 Great Chedis

There are about 100 *chedis* in the grounds of Wat Pho **(left)**, but the four most important, in the western courtyard, are the Great Chedis, which enshrine royal ashes and remains of sacred Buddha images. The *chedis* are decorated with porcelain mosaic.

6 The Bot

This ordination hall is Wat Pho's largest build-ing. Inside, the base of the large bronze image of Buddha contains the ashes of Rama I.

7 Farang Guards

Adding a whimsical touch to this temple of learning are huge stone caricatures of Westerners, *farang* in Thai, wearing top hats **(left)**. These guards stand beside the gateways to the inner courtyard of the temple.

8 Phra Rabiang

When Rama I originally built the temple, he installed 1,200 Buddha images from northern Thailand. Today, around 400 of these golden Buddha statues line Phra Rabiang, a double cloister outside the ordination hall.

10 Monks and Their Guti

Away from the most popular attractions in the complex, visitors might see monks who work at the temple **(below)**. They live in *gutis* (simple rooms) in a compound to the south of the temple.

🔟 ⭐ Bangkok's Canals

In the 19th century, Bangkok was known as the "Venice of the East," since all transportation was by canal. Today, most of the canals to the east of the Chao Phraya River have been filled in to create new roads. However, the area to the west remains much as it was in the 1800s, with a network of waterways spreading out into the countryside. Here, visitors can get a taste of canalside life and visit attractions such as Wat Arun and the Royal Barge Museum.

① Floating Vendors

Floating vendors still go from house to house in Thonburi, selling anything from hot food to plastic buckets. There is a better chance of seeing them in the morning.

NEED TO KNOW

Khlong Mon: **MAP A5**

Khlong Bangkok Noi: **MAP A2**

Khlong Bangkok Yai: **MAP B6**

Chao Phraya River: **MAP B5**

■ To tour the canals, either hire a longtail boat (about B800–1,000 per hour) from any pier, join an organized tour on a larger boat, or take the Saen Saeb Express.

■ Organized tours usually provide refreshments or make a stop where you can buy drinks and food from floating vendors.

③ Khlong Mon

Branching off from the river just north of Wat Arun, this canal leads to an orchid farm where visitors step ashore for a look around before continuing to explore the canal.

④ Boats

It is great fun to sit at a riverside café and watch the pageant of vessels flow by. Huge barges chug downstream, while small ferries nip from bank to bank, and longtail boats with bright awnings **(above)** roar past.

② Traditional Thai Houses

Traditional houses **(below)** line the canals to the west of the Chao Phraya River. Set on stilts, they usually have an open veranda and pitched roofs.

⑤ Wat Arun

Established by Rama I, Wat Arun *(see pp30–31)* is known as the Temple of the Dawn. Its highlights are the five *prangs* (towers), encrusted with colorful pieces of porcelain.

Map of Bangkok's canals

Royal Barge Museum 6

This museum *(see p96)* contains a fabulous display of ornamented royal barges **(right)**, which are about 165 ft (50 m) long. Also on display are dioramas of robes worn by royal rowers and information on the use of the barges that appear in royal processions on the river.

Khlong Bangkok Noi 7

Though it is now termed a *khlong*, or canal, this waterway *(see p98)* was once the main channel of the Chao Phraya River. Near its entrance is the Royal Barge Museum and a little farther on is Wat Suwannaram, which has some rich murals.

Saen Saeb Canal 8

This canal **(right)** is quite useful for reaching the Old City from Downtown. The Saen Saeb Express boats run from Saphan Phanfa Lela to Pratunam, and beyond if you transfer.

Khlong Bangkok Yai 10

Popular with tour boats, this canal passes several temples, including Wat Kalayanamit *(see p98)*, which has a huge Buddha image, and Wat Pak Nam, famous for its amulets. Many boats also stop at a snake farm and the floating market along Khlong Dao Khanong.

Chao Phraya – River of Kings 9

Without the Chao Phraya River **(below)**, there would be no Bangkok. Named for the founder of the Chakri dynasty, Chao Phraya Chakri *(see p38)*, the river has always been the lifeblood of the nation, providing an aquatic highway for a range of boats.

RIDING THE CHAO PHRAYA EXPRESS

River buses are a great way to see the Chao Phraya and beat the traffic. The central section from Sathorn (Central) pier upstream to Phra Athit takes around 30 minutes, passing by several sights, such as the Church of Santa Cruz *(see p98)*, Wat Arun, Wat Phra Kaeo *(see pp12–13)*, and Wat Rakhang *(see p98)*. The website www.chaophraya expressboat.com has more information.

Following pages Wat Pho's elaborate Scripture Hall

TOP 10 ⭐ Damnoen Saduak Floating Market

Today, the many waterways of Bangkok's once-extensive canal network have been filled in to make new roads, but the Damnoen Saduak Floating Market still remains in operation, namely for tourists. Visitors can explore the labyrinth of lively canals here, sampling fresh, local food from vendors dressed in traditional blue attire. Various souvenirs are also on offer.

1 Fruits
Many of the *sampans* (simple, square-ended rowing boats) on the canals here sell freshly picked pomelos, bananas, rose apples, and jackfruit **(above)**.

2 Bridge
There are plenty of opportunities for taking pictures while exploring by boat, but the classic view of the floating market, busy with boats, is from the bridge at Ton Kem Market.

OTHER FLOATING MARKETS

Damnoen Saduak gets the lion's share of visitors to floating markets, but there are other locations in and around Bangkok where similar markets operate, if only once a week. These include Amphawa, Tha Kha, Lam Phya, Don Wai, Wat Sai, and Taling Chan. The last two are near the center of Bangkok, but are exclusively for tourists.

5 Ton Kem Market
What is referred to as Damnoen Saduak Floating Market is actually three separate markets, the biggest being Ton Kem Market on Khlong Damnoen Saduak **(below)**. This market is very popular with both tour groups and vendors, so the canal often gets jammed with boats.

3 Fruit Orchards
To add variety to a visit to the floating market, many tour groups include a visit to an orchard to sample ripe fruit. Some orchards also keep harmless pythons, which tourists can drape round their necks for a souvenir photo.

4 Boat Noodles
It is a minor miracle that cooks can prepare a tasty bowl of *gooaydteeo rua* (boat noodles), in a small boat and serve it without spilling a drop **(below)**. These are so popular that noodle shops often display their dishes in a boat.

8 Boats

Most vendors paddle around in *sampans*, which are easily maneuvered and ideal for displaying goods for sale **(left)**. The tourists, however, are propelled around the canals in longtail boats. These boats can be noisy but will offer protection from the elements and can cover a big area in a short time.

9 Boat Vendors

The *sampans* that the vendors paddle along the canals provide no protection from the elements, so most vendors wear a *ngob* – a traditional hat that ingeniously allows for ventilation. Many also wear a type of collarless denim shirt typical in rural Thailand.

6 Hia Kui Market

A short way south of Ton Kem is Hia Kui Market, which offers a more local shopping experience. The banks of the canal are dotted with souvenir shops where some group tours stop for mementos.

7 Khun Pitak Market

On a smaller canal south of Hia Kui, Khun Pitak is the least crowded of the three markets, but it is still a bustling place early in the morning when the locals buy fresh produce and spices.

NEED TO KNOW

MAP S2 ■ 62 miles (100 km) SW of Bangkok ■ AC minibus or bus from Bangkok's Southern Bus Terminal

■ To enjoy the market before busloads of tourists arrive (*usually around* 9–10am). Stay overnight in a local guesthouse and get out on the canals in the early morning.

■ Most guided tours include refreshments, but there are a large number of vendors on the canals selling food and drink for independent travelers.

10 Souvenirs

With busloads of tourists arriving in Damnoen Saduak every morning, many locals operate souvenir stalls on the banks of the canals, selling traditional hats **(above)**, silk purses, carved soaps, and, of course, colorful postcards of the market.

TOP 10 ⭐ Chatuchak Weekend Market

Chatuchak Market, held every Saturday and Sunday, is the biggest market in Thailand. An estimated quarter of a million people visit this veritable shopaholic's paradise each day. The vast site has more than 15,000 stalls, but products are grouped by theme into a series of numbered sections, making it easy to find specific items.

1 Home Decor

Items to beautify your home (left) can be found in sections 2 to 7. If you wish to buy bulky items, you can ship them home via a number of shipping companies located in the market.

2 Crafts

Thailand is renowned all over the world for its handicrafts, including woodcarvings, basketware, lacquerware, ceramics, silk, silverware, and musical instruments. Such items can be found in section 8 of the market, where, with a little bit of luck, all the gifts you may need for your friends and family can be purchased in one go.

3 Plants

In sections 3 and 4 of the market you can pick up a young fruit tree or a rose bush, a sweet-smelling jasmine plant, or a delicate orchid. There are also a few stalls which sell fertilizer, flower pots, and gardening tools.

4 Chatuchak Park

If you need a break from the crowds, head to the adjacent Chatuchak Park (below), just north of the market. Running the length of the park is an artificial lake. Also located nearby is the Bangkok Butterfly Garden (see p55) in Rotfai Park.

(see p55)

NEED TO KNOW

MAP T5 ■ Thanon Phaholyothin ■ Skytrain Mo Chit, MRT Subway Chatuchak Park or Kampaeng Phet ■ www.chatuchakmarket.org

Open 6am–6pm Sat & Sun

■ Go to Chatuchak in the morning to avoid the worst of the heat. Bargaining is expected, and some vendors will reduce their initial prices by half.

■ Simple maps are handed out free but serious shoppers should pick up Nancy Chandler's map of Bangkok, available at many bookstores and hotels.

■ To eat and drink in air-conditioned comfort, head to the Dream Section, which has several modern restaurants, offering varied cuisines.

7 Central Clock Tower

The tall clock tower **(left)** in the heart of the market is a useful landmark because it is visible from many areas. If you get lost, head for this clock tower, from where it should be easier to find your way.

ENDANGERED SPECIES

Unfortunately, Thailand is a major conduit for the sale of endangered species coming from neighboring countries. Several raids on dealers in Chatuchak Weekend Market have revealed animals being kept in awful conditions, and while casual visitors are never likely to see them, this illegal trade still continues underground.

10 Antiques

Located in section 26 of the market, antiques on sale include furniture, paintings, Buddha images **(left)**, lamps, jewelry, clocks, and carvings. Take extra care when considering a purchase as fake antiques are common; note that genuine antiques will need the appropriate documentation for customs clearance.

5 Books

Bibliophiles will love section 1, which has remaindered art books stacked beside collectible first editions and back issues of magazines. It is best visited last as the weight of purchases may discourage further exploration of the market.

8 Artists

There is an excellent art market located in section 7. Here, visitors will find small studios producing good-value paintings as well as higher-end pieces of art. Artists can be viewed at work on original pieces, and it is also possible to commission reproductions.

6 Food and Drink Stalls

More than 400 food and drink stalls are scattered throughout the market. Many of these stalls specialize in only one expertly cooked dish, so snacking here can be a superb gourmet experience.

9 Clothing and Accessories

The market houses around 5,000 stalls that sell either clothes or fabric **(right)**, as well as fashion accessories. Most of them are in sections 12, 14, 16, 18, and 20. With rock-bottom prices, these are some of the most popular and crowded sections of the market.

TOP10 ⭐ Jim Thompson House

Jim Thompson, an American businessman who came to Bangkok in 1945, is credited with having revived the Thai art of silk weaving. His traditional Thai house contains a fantastic selection of Southeast Asian antiques, paintings, and sculptures. Surrounded by a lush garden, the large house has actually been constructed by combining six smaller teak houses, most of which are over 200 years old.

4 Dining Room
Like the master bedroom, the dining room also enjoys lovely views of the garden. The room features several items of Ming porcelain as well as some fine paintings. The dining table, which consists of two mahjong tables put together, is laid out for a meal as it might have been during the days of Jim Thompson.

1 Drawing Room
This large and airy room looks out onto a terrace and is decorated in orange and red colors **(above)**. It houses a 14th-century sandstone head of the Buddha and wooden carvings of Burmese figures set in illuminated alcoves.

2 Jataka Paintings
Near the entrance are paintings depicting scenes from the *Jataka* tales, which show the previous incarnations of Buddha. The panels were painted in the early 1800s.

5 Spirit House
Located near the canal, the spirit house **(left)** generally has ritualistic offerings of fresh fruit, flowers and incense to pacify and appease the spirits of the land on which the house stands.

3 Master Bedroom
With a great view over the garden, this room is filled with sculptures, paintings of the *Jataka* tales, and photographs of Jim Thompson.

6 The Garden
Surrounding the house is a garden with cooling pools and dense tropical vegetation **(below)** including flowers, banana plants, and palm trees.

JIM THOMPSON'S DISAPPEARANCE

On Easter Day, 1967, Jim Thompson went out walking in the Cameron Highlands in Malaysia. He was never seen again. His former role in the Office of Strategic Services (OSS), a predecessor of the CIA, fueled suspicion that he was abducted by Vietnamese communists, though others suspect he was hit by a truck and that the driver buried the remains.

8 Ban Khrua Silk Weavers

Thompson chose this location beside Khlong Saen Saeb because a silk weavers' community **(left)** lived at Ban Khrua, on the opposite bank. This made it easy for him to oversee their work.

7 Traditional Teak Houses

The roofs of these six traditional stilted houses are steeply pitched for ventilation, and the walls lean inward to create a sense of height.

9 Dvaravati Buddha Torso

Probably the most significant example of early Asian art at the complex, this headless Buddha torso, made of limestone during the Dvaravati period (6th–9th centuries), was found in Lopburi Province. The statue is on display in the garden that surrounds the house.

10 Burmese Carvings

These intricate carvings display a high level of artistic ability. Jim Thompson's extensive collection of wooden figures includes images of *nats* **(below)**, animist spirits that were incorporated into Buddhism when it developed in Myanmar.

Floorplan of Jim Thompson House

Master Bedroom · 3
1 Drawing Room
4 Dining Room

Burmese 10 Carvings

Key to Floorplan
▪ First floor
▪ Second floor

Dvaravati 9 Buddha Torso
Jataka 2 Paintings
Spirit 5 House

NEED TO KNOW

MAP P2 ▪ 6 Soi Kasem San 2, Rama I Road ▪ 02 216 7368 ▪ Skytrain National Stadium ▪ www.jimthompson house.com

Open 10am–6pm daily, last guided tour at 5pm

Adm B200

▪ Ignore any touts hanging around the house who tell you it is closed; they just want to take you shopping elsewhere so they can get a commission.

▪ The branch of Jim Thompson Silk, located on the grounds, sells small souvenir items such as ties and purses, while the Jim Thompson Center for the Arts upstairs hosts fascinating temporary exhibitions.

▪ The enticing wine bar and restaurant *(open 10am–5pm & 6–11pm daily)* offer repose next to a tranquil lotus pond.

🔟 ⭐ Wat Arun

Wat Arun is named for Aruna, the Indian god of dawn, because General Taksin arrived here at sunrise on an October day in 1767 to establish Thonburi as Siam's new capital. With its prominent *prangs* (towers), the temple shows a strong Khmer influence. All the *prangs* are ornamentally encrusted with colorful broken porcelain.

NEED TO KNOW

MAP B5 ■ 34 Arun Amarin Road, Thonburi ■ 02 891 2185 ■ Cross-river ferry from Tha Tien Pier

Open 8am–6pm daily

Adm B100

■ Viewing Wat Arun for the first time may invoke a sense of *déjà vu*. Its silhouette has been used in the official logo of the Tourism Authority of Thailand.

■ Although strolling food and drink vendors do occasionally look for business at the temple, there is no permanent café at the temple, so it's always best to carry a bottle of water with you around the complex.

■ If you visit in the late afternoon, in time to enjoy views of the temple at sunset, you can pause for refreshment at one of the cafés on the east bank of the river.

1 Stairs on Central Prang

The steep stairs up the central *prang* represent the difficulties humans face when trying to attain enlightenment. They lead up to a terrace with a view, but the upper stairway is often closed.

2 Chinese Guards

Steps lead up to the first terrace, and each set of steps is guarded by Chinese figures that may have arrived as ballast on ships. There are also statues of many mythical creatures on the terrace.

3 River View

It may be called the Temple of Dawn, but Wat Arun's best view is seen at sunset from the east bank of the river **(below)**. There are cafés and restaurants around Tha Tien from where you can watch the sun slip down behind the temple's soaring *prang*.

4 Central Prang

The central *prang* **(above)** was extended to its current height of 266 ft (81 m) by Rama III (r. 1824–51). It represents Mount Meru, the abode of the gods in Hindu and Buddhist cosmology. It is topped with a thunderbolt, the weapon of the god Indra, who has also been depicted riding the three-headed elephant Erawan in niches on the *prang*.

⑤ Ceramic Details

The colorful ceramics **(above)** that cover the *prang* are an early form of recycling. In the 1800s, Chinese trading ships carried broken porcelain as ballast. When offloaded, it was used as decoration.

⑥ Kinnaris

Tucked away in small coves on the second level of the central *prang* are *kinnaris*, creatures that are half-bird, half-woman. *Kinnaris* are just one of the many Thai mythical creatures *(see p15)* depicted at the temple.

⑧ The Bot

The Buddha image in the *bot* or the ordination hall *(see p40)* was apparently molded by Rama II (r.1809–24) himself, and his ashes are buried in the base of this statue **(left)**. The murals were created during the reign of Rama V.

⑩ Symbolic Levels

The central *prang* has three symbolic levels. The base stands for *Traiphum*, all realms of existence in the Buddhist universe; the middle, *Tavatimsa*, where desires are gratified; the top, *Devaphum*, six heavens within seven realms of happiness.

⑦ Decoration of Minor Prangs

Representing the four great seas, these smaller *prangs* are supported by demons and monkeys. Each has a niche with a statue of Phra Pai, the god of wind, on a white horse.

⑨ Mondops

Between the four corner *prangs* are placed four *mondops* or shrines **(right)**. Each holds a Buddha statue from a key stage of his life – birth (north), meditation (east), preaching (south), and entering Nirvana (west).

TOP 10 ⭐ Ayutthaya

From the 14th century, Ayutthaya was the capital of an independent kingdom until the city was sacked by the Burmese in 1767. It was never restored as a capital city. Today, Ayutthaya is a UNESCO World Heritage Site, and its ruins give a sense of the city's former size and glory as well as offering an insight into Thailand's cultural heritage.

2 Wat Thammikarat

One of the park's most atmospheric temples (left), it has the ruins of an octagonal *chedi* (stupa), a *wihan*, and a fearsome *singha* (see p13).

3 Ayutthaya Historical Study Center

This center depicts the city's history and trading relations, with models of ships and other historical objects. It also has a model of Wat Phra Si Sanphet, a once great temple that is now in ruins.

1 Wihan Phra Mongkhon Bophit

This *wihan* (assembly hall) was built in the 1950s to shelter a very large bronze Buddha image that dates back to the 15th century.

4 Wat Phra Mahathat

An important temple during Ayutthaya's heyday, it is one of the most evocative sights in the city (left). It has *prangs* (towers) leaning at precarious angles and a stone Buddha head encased by the roots of a banyan tree.

NEED TO KNOW

MAP T1 ▪ 53 miles (85 km) N of Bangkok

Chao Sam Phraya National Museum: open 9am–4pm Wed–Sun; adm B150

Ayutthaya Historical Study Center: open 9am–5pm daily; adm B100

▪ Most temples are open 8am–6pm daily, and entry usually costs B50 (some temples are free).

▪ Some tour agencies include a boat trip either to or from Ayutthaya, the ideal way to approach the historic city.

▪ The best way to get around is by bike, though many visitors opt for tuk tuks or an air-conditioned minibus.

▪ Malakor restaurant, in front of Wat Ratchaburana, serves both Thai and Western dishes.

5 Chao Sam Phraya National Museum

Most of Ayutthaya's precious artifacts, including gold Buddha images, were either taken by the invading Burmese or looters. A few remaining items are on show here **(right)**.

6 Wat Phra Si Sanphet

Once Ayutthaya's most glorious temple, all that is left of Wat Phra Si Sanphet **(below)** today, are three Sri Lankan-style *chedis* alongside the ruins of the royal palace. The *chedis* contain ashes of Ayutthayan kings and are the park's highlight.

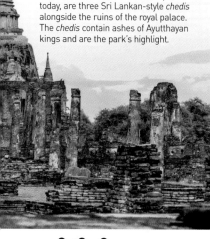

A SHORT HISTORY OF AYUTTHAYA

Ayutthaya was founded by King Ramathibodi I in 1350. Over the next four centuries, the kingdom came to dominate the region now known as Thailand, apart from in the north (where the Kingdom of Lanna maintained its independence). Traders from Europe returned home with tales of a highly organized and sophisticated society. The kingdom's end was as sudden as its beginning, and its capital was completely abandoned after being sacked by the Burmese in 1767.

10 Wat Ratchaburana

Opposite Wat Phra Mahathat, this temple was built in 1424 by King Borommaracha II, and its main structure is a Khmer-style *prang*. In 1957, the crypt beneath the *prang* was opened by robbers, who made off with a horde of gold artifacts. The few items they did not take are now on display in the Chao Sam Phraya National Museum. The crypt can be reached by a steep staircase, where there are beautiful frescoes.

Map of Ayutthaya

8 Wang Luang

Constructed in the 15th century by King Borommatrailokanat *(see p35)*, this royal palace had enough stable space for over 100 elephants. It was razed to the ground by the Burmese and only the foundations remain.

7 Wat Lokaya Sutharam

This temple's highlight is a huge, whitewashed Reclining Buddha **(right)**, exposed to the elements. The pillars around it once supported a wooden hall which sheltered the image.

9 Wat Phra Ram

Wat Phra Ram is one of Ayutthaya's oldest temples, originally built in 1369. The main *prang*, decorated with Buddha images and mythical creatures like *nagas* and *garudas (see p13)*, was added during the 15th century.

Sights In and Around Ayutthaya

1 Bang Pa-In
15 miles (24 km) S of Ayutthaya ■ Open 8am–4pm daily ■ Adm

Included on many tours of Ayutthaya, this former royal summer retreat is an eclectic mix of Thai and Western architectural styles. The Aisawan Thipphaya-at pavilion that sits on a lake is its most photographed building.

2 Wat Yai Chai Mongkol
1 mile (2 km) E of Ayutthaya ■ Open 8am–5pm daily ■ Adm

Aisawan Thipphaya-at pavilion at Bang Pa-In

The main features of this temple include a huge *chedi* (stupa) erected by King Naresuan, a host of saffron-robed, laterite Buddha images that surround it, and a large Reclining Buddha set in the northeast corner of the temple grounds.

3 Wat Phanan Choeng
S of Ayutthaya ■ Open 8am–5pm daily ■ Adm

Particularly popular with Chinese worshippers because of a shrine to a Chinese princess, this temple dates back to the 14th century, and has been renovated over the years. Its centerpiece is a 62-ft- (19-m-) tall, seated bronze image of the Buddha.

4 Lopburi
44 miles (70 km) N of Ayutthaya

One of Thailand's oldest towns, Lopburi was an important center of Dvaravati culture from the 6th century onwards. Both King Narai the Great and Rama IV *(see p38)* used it as a second capital, and Narai's palace is well worth a visit.

5 Chantarakasem Palace Museum
NE corner of Ayutthaya ■ Open 8:30am–4pm Wed–Sun ■ Adm

Ayutthaya's oldest museum displays a throne platform that belonged to Rama IV, some beautiful ceramics and Buddha images, and a collection of cannons and muskets.

6 Wat Na Phra Mane
N of Ayutthaya ■ Open 8am–5pm daily ■ Adm

This temple was less badly damaged than most by the invading Burmese, who used it as a base during the siege. It is therefore one of the most interesting to explore. Inside is a large *bot* (ordination hall), which displays some fine architectural features, and a small *wihan* (assembly hall) which houses a rare Dvaravati stone Buddha.

Statue in Wat Phanan Choeng

7 Wat Phu Khao Thong
1 mile (2 km) NW of Ayutthaya

Also known as the Golden Mount, this temple's main feature is its *chedi*. It is possible to climb part of the way up the structure to get a panoramic view of the rice fields.

8 Wat Puthaisawan
S of Ayutthaya

Located across the river from central Ayutthaya, the temple has a restored 14th-century *prang* (tower), which is surrounded by cloisters that are packed with Buddha images.

9 Wat Chai Wattanaram
W of Ayutthaya

Built in the 17th century and restored in the late 20th century, Wat Chai Wattanaram is modeled on Angkor Wat in Cambodia, with a central *prang* surrounded by eight smaller ones.

10 St. Joseph's Cathedral
S of Ayutthaya

A cathedral was built here in the 17th century to accommodate the needs of foreign merchants, who were not permitted to enter the city center except by invitation. The cathedral was renovated in the 19th century and is still functional.

Interior of St. Joseph's Cathedral

KING NARAI THE GREAT (R.1656–88)

Narai is best remembered for his warming of diplomatic relations with Western countries, his sending of missions to European courts, and his selection of a foreigner, Constantine Phaulkon, as his principal advisor. It was from reports by European merchants of this era that Ayutthaya became known in the west for its richness and splendor. Phaulkon encouraged Narai to balance Dutch interests in the kingdom by inviting a French delegation to visit. However, many Siamese suspected, quite correctly as it turned out, that the French mission's main objective was to convert the king to Christianity, and on Narai's death French officials and troops were banished from Ayutthaya.

King Narai the Great was a usurper, like most kings of Ayutthaya, and he deposed his uncle, Si Suthammaracha, to take the throne.

TOP 10 KINGS OF AYUTTHAYA

1 **Ramathibodi** (r.1351–69)

2 **Borommaracha I** (r.1370–88)

3 **Borommaracha II** (r.1424–48)

4 **Borommatrailokanat** (r.1448–88)

5 **Ramathibodi II** (r.1491–1529)

6 **Naresuan** (r.1590–1605)

7 **Prasat Thong** (r.1629–56)

8 **Narai** (r.1656–88)

9 **Phra Phetracha** (r.1688–1703)

10 **Phumintharacha** (r.1758–67)

The Top 10
of Everything

The bustling interior of Central World
shopping mall

🔟 Moments in History

① 1767: Ayutthaya Overrun by the Burmese

After 400 years of being one of Asia's most powerful empires, the Kingdom of Ayutthaya *(see pp32–5)* was invaded by Burmese troops in 1767. Though the Burmese were expelled within a year, Ayutthaya was deemed unsafe as a capital and General Taksin chose Thonburi as the new capital of Siam (now Thailand).

② 1782: Bangkok Founded

Just 15 years later, a rebellion against Taksin's autocratic rule led to his demise. He was succeeded by General Chao Phraya Chakri who established the Chakri dynasty and acquired the official title of Rama I. On assuming the throne, his first action was to move the capital east across the river to Bangkok.

③ 1851: Rama IV Crowned

After 27 years as a monk, Mongkut acceded to the throne to become Rama IV of the Chakri dynasty. Thais regard him as the man who began to modernize Siam, particularly through treaties that opened the country to trade with the West.

④ 1868: Rama V Crowned

Chulalongkorn, son of Rama IV, succeeded his father as Rama V of the Chakri Dynasty when he was only 15 years old. He ruled for over 40 years and is credited with keeping Siam free from the clutches of

Rama V, King of Siam (r.1868–1910)

colonial powers such as England and France, which were carving up Southeast Asia at the time.

⑤ 1893: First Railroad Line

Rama V carried on his father's programme of modernization, and in 1893 the country's first railroad line opened, stretching just 14 miles (22 km) to Pak Nam. The network was later extended to the south, north, and northeast of the country.

Rama IV, crowned in 1851

⑥ 1932: End to Absolute Monarchy

The absolute power of the Siamese monarchy was ended by a bloodless coup in 1932, and a constitutional monarchy was established. It brought the military to power, setting the stage for the string of coups and counter-coups that has dominated Thailand's politics since.

1946: Rama IX Ascends the Throne

After the death of his brother King Ananda, who was shot in the head while in bed, King Bhumibol Adulyadej took over the throne as Rama IX. He reigned for 70 years, until his death in 2016.

8 1992: Military Government Ousted

In 1992, Thais demonstrated their displeasure publicly following a military coup. After the army gunned down many citizens on the streets of Bangkok, Rama IX intervened, resulting in the self-proclaimed Prime Minister, General Suchinda Kraprayoon, making a hasty exit and democracy being restored.

Protests against the military coup

2011: Thailand's First Female Prime Minister

Yingluck Shinawatra was elected Thailand's first female Prime Minister, widely viewed as a proxy for her brother. She was deposed in a 2014 coup by General Prayut Chan-o-cha, who went on to oversee the succession of Rama X, King Vajiralongkorn, in 2016.

2020: Student Protests

University protests against Prime Minister Prayut Chan-o-Cha, who came to power as part of a military coup in 2014, began in 2020. Initially aimed at restoring a democratically elected government, the protests later came to encompass other issues, such as abortion rights and education reform.

TOP 10 FAMOUS THAIS

Conjoined twins Chang and Eng Bunker

1 Chang and Eng Bunker
Born in Thailand (originally Siam) in 1811, these conjoined twins were known around the world as the original "Siamese Twins".

2 Plaek Pibulsonggram
Prime Minister and military dictator for around 15 years, Pibulsonggram changed the country's name from Siam to Thailand in 1939.

3 Apsara Hongsakula
Crowned Miss Universe in 1965, Apsara Hongsakula was the first of three Thai women to win the accolade.

4 Khaosai Galaxy
The "Thai Tyson", Khaosai was WBA Super Flyweight champion from 1984 to 1992, defending his title 19 times.

5 Kukrit Pramoj
Thailand's 13th Prime Minister (1975–6) was honored in 1985 as National Artist for his literary works.

6 Anand Panyarachun
Serving twice as Prime Minister in the early 1990s, Panyarachun made overdue reforms to the Thai constitution in 1996.

7 Sirikit
Thailand's current queen mother is universally beloved and her birthday is celebrated as Mother's Day.

8 Thongchai McIntyre
Known as "Bird," Thailand's biggest pop idol also has a film and TV acting career.

9 Chalermchai Kositpipat
The Buddhism-inspired works of one of Thailand's greatest contemporary artists include an entire temple in Chiang Rai

10 Jay Fai
Described as "Mozart of the noodle pan", Fai oversees a Michelin-starred street food stall in Bangkok.

🔟 Buddhist Temples

1 Wat Bowoniwet
Built in 1826, this temple has gained significance for being the place where Thai kings are ordained and as one of the main bases of Buddhism in Thailand. The murals inside feature some unusual themes, such as horse racing in England and Dutch windmills (see p72).

Wat Suthat's bronze Buddha

2 Wat Suthat
One of the most important temples in Thailand, Wat Suthat (see p71) was built in the early 1800s to house a 26-ft- (8-m-) tall bronze Buddha image from Sukhothai, which sits in the wihan, surrounded by murals. The galleries around the wihan hold over 150 Buddha images. The towering Sao Ching Cha, or Giant Swing, once used in a Brahmin cere-mony, stands in front of the temple.

3 Wat Traimit
This rebuilt temple (see p76) located in Chinatown is firmly fixed on the tourist trail because of the Golden Buddha, a 13th-century Sukhothai-style image made of gleaming solid gold.

4 Wat Suwannaram
On the Bangkok Noi canal in Thonburi, near the Royal Barge Museum, this Ayutthaya-style temple (see p98) was built during the reign of King Taksin. Step into the main building of the temple to see some of best temple murals in the country, including depictions of Westerners from the Ayutthaya era.

5 Wat Mahathat
Prince Mongkut was a monk in the Wat Mahathat temple (see p72) for 12 years before he became Rama IV (see p38). Today, the Wat Mahathat complex serves as the headquarters of the Mahachulalongkorn Buddhist University and also houses the reputed Vipassana Meditation Center.

6 Wat Saket and the Golden Mount
Built by Rama I in the late 1700s, this temple (see p70) has some excellent murals and a peaceful atmosphere. The main attraction, though, is the view of the Old City from the Golden Mount, a 250-ft (76-m) high man-made hill inside the temple.

7 Wat Benjamabophit
MAP E2 ■ Nakhon Pathom Road ■ 02 282 9686 ■ Open 7am–6pm daily ■ Adm

The last major temple built in Bangkok (between 1899 and 1911), this is also known as the Marble Temple because of its extraordinary Carrara marble bot. The ashes of Rama V are buried beneath the golden Buddha image inside the temple.

Wat Benjamabophit

Golden *chedi* at Wat Phra Kaeo

8 Wat Phra Kaeo

For many visitors, the highlight of their stay in Bangkok is a visit to Wat Phra Kaeo *(see pp12–13)*, to see beautiful examples of Buddhist art and architecture. This sacred temple features a glittering array of *chedis*, libraries, mausoleums, and the small jadeite Buddha that is the nation's greatest treasure.

9 Wat Ratchabophit

A blend of local and Western architecture, this temple *(see p72)* was built in the late 19th century by Rama V *(see p38)*, and its design was inspired by the circular *chedi* (stupa) at Nakhon Pathom. The temple's 141-ft (43-m) *chedi* is surrounded by cloisters, into which are set a *wihan* and a *bot* designed like an Italian Gothic chapel.

Detail of Wat Ratchabophit

10 Wat Pho

Bangkok's biggest and oldest temple, Wat Pho *(see pp18–19)* is known across the globe for its main attraction, the 150-ft- (46-m-) long Reclining Buddha. This *wat* is more typical of temples countrywide than Wat Phra Kaeo because it has resident monks who live in simple lodgings within the complex. It also runs a respected school of massage.

TOP 10 ELEMENTS OF A THAI TEMPLE COMPOUND

1 Wihan
The main assembly hall of a temple, where the head abbot gives sermons and people come to pray.

2 Bot
The ordination hall, which is usually smaller than the *wihan*. Highly decorated, it is off-limits to women.

3 Chedi
These dome-shaped religious monuments, or stupas, have relics sealed within their base.

4 Novices
Young men live as novices in the temple before being ordained as monks.

5 Ho Trai
The library in each temple stores sacred texts and is often raised off the ground to avoid flood damage.

6 Guti
These are the monks' living quarters in a temple complex – sometimes a small, austure wooden room set on stilts.

7 Murals
Temple murals depict incidents from the life of the Buddha, and some record scenes of Thai daily life.

8 Buddha Images
Usually the most highly valued Buddha image is placed in the *wihan*. Other images may sit or stand in the *bot* or cloisters.

9 Monks
These are holy men who follow the Buddha's teachings and advise lay people on their problems.

10 Bodhi Tree
This tree *(Ficus religiosa)* symbolizes Enlightenment, as the Buddha is said to have been sitting beneath a Bodhi tree when he attained Nirvana.

A Buddha's head in a Bodhi tree

🔟 Museums and Art Galleries

1 National Museum

An accurate overview of the evolution of Thai culture is laid out in the National Museum (see pp16–17) through exquisite Sukhothai, Ayutthaya, Rattanakosin, and Lanna artifacts. Don't miss the Ramkhamhaeng stone, bearing the oldest known inscription using the Thai alphabet, the Royal Funeral Chariots Gallery, and the Buddhaisawan Chapel.

2 Royal Barge Museum

Housed inside a dry-dock warehouse, this museum (see p96) features eight gleaming barges, each nearly 165 ft (50 m) long, that are used only for special royal events. The biggest, most important barge, *Suphannahongse*, carries the king.

Royal Barge Museum

3 National Gallery

Both traditional and contemporary Thai art are featured at this gallery (see p72). There are also many temporary exhibitions. Temple banners are displayed in the section upstairs, and there is an art market in the courtyard each weekend.

4 Museum of Contemporary Art

MAP T5 ■ Vibhavadi Rangsit Road, Chatuchak ■ 02 016 5666 ■ Open 10am–5pm Tue–Fri, 11am–6pm Sat & Sun ■ Adm ■ www.moca bangkok.com

This modernist five-story museum is the pride of Thai contemporary artists, with more than 800 pieces on permanent display. Entire galleries are dedicated to the works of Thailand's most famous artists, including Chalermchai Kositpipat and Tawan Dachanee.

5 SAC Gallery

MAP T6 ■ 160 3 Soi Sukhumvit 39 ■ Open 10am–6pm Tue–Sat ■ www. sac.gallery

Housed in a sleek modern building overlooking a verdant courtyard, this art gallery showcases the work of some of the best contemporary artists from Southeast Asia.

Traditional houses surrounded by lush greens in Suan Pakkad Palace Museum

6 Suan Pakkad Palace Museum

A compound of traditional Thai houses, Suan Pakkad Palace Museum *(see p86)* is an excellent example of Thai architecture. The houses contain antique paintings, carvings, and a stunning display of masks used in *khon* (masked theater).

7 The Queen's Gallery

MAP D3 ■ **101 Ratchadamnoen Klang Road** ■ **02 281 5360 1** ■ **Open 10am–7pm Thu–Tue** ■ **Adm** ■ **www.queengallery.org**

Established in 2003 at the request of Queen Sirikit, this gallery occupies a massive 39,825 sq ft (3,700 sq m) of exhibition space. The Queen wanted to showcase leading examples of Thai visual art. The gallery's shop stocks an interesting range of glossy art books and T-shirts featuring contemporary art.

8 Charmchuri Art Gallery

MAP P3 ■ **Chulalongkorn University, Phaya Thai Road** ■ **02 218 3709** ■ **Open 10am–7pm Mon–Fri, noon–6pm Sat & Sun** ■ **www.charmchuriartgallery.chula.ac.th**

Located on the campus grounds near Siam Square at Bangkok's prestigious Chulalongkorn University is the Charmchuri Art Gallery. It features a vibrant selection of artworks created by students and professors from the university, as well as by upcoming and established Thai and international artists.

9 Bangkok Art & Culture Centre

MAP P2 ■ **Corner of Phaya Thai and Rama I roads** ■ **02 214 6630** ■ **www.bacc.or.th**

Housing several galleries of contemporary art on its upper floors, connected by spiralling ramps like New York's Guggenheim Museum, the prestigious Bangkok Art & Culture Centre *(see p62)* covers all media, from the visual arts to music and design.

10 Museum of Siam

Highly imaginative, this interactive museum *(see p72)* covers the history, art, culture and traditions of Thailand from the distant past to the present with audio-visual and traditional displays. It's a museum that kids will really love.

Interior of the Museum of Siam

🔟 Spas

① Banyan Tree Spa
MAP Q5 ■ Banyan Tree Hotel, South Sathorn Road ■ 02 679 1052 ■ Open 10am–8pm daily ■ www.banyantreespa.com

Located on the 39th floor of the Banyan Tree Hotel, this deluxe spa has fantastic views and offers an extensive menu of services, including the 150-minute Royal Banyan package, comprising a herbal pouch massage, a face massage, and a herbal bath.

② Oriental Spa
MAP M5 ■ Oriental Hotel ■ 02 659 9000/ 7440 ■ Open 10am–8pm daily ■ www.mandarinoriental.com

This spa is an oasis of calm, combining ancient Asian healing philosophies with modern techniques. The traditional Thai teak building is the ideal place to unwind with a massage, floral mask facial, or mud wrap.

③ Anantara Siam Spa
MAP Q3 ■ Anantara Siam Hotel, Ratchadamri Road ■ 02 126 8866 ■ Open 10am–8pm daily ■ www.anantara.com

Each suite in this spa is decorated in traditional Thai style, and some have large Roman bathtubs. The treatments include a Japanese-style bamboo massage and specific therapies for men.

Interiors of Anantara Siam Spa

Chi, The Spa, at the Shangri-La

④ Chi, The Spa
MAP M6 ■ Shangri-La Hotel ■ 02 236 7777 ■ Open 10am–9pm Wed–Sun ■ www.shangri-la.com/en

With its minimalist design, this spa facility is nothing less than a sanctuary of tranquility. The suites are some of Bangkok's largest, offering an array of treatments designed to restore *chi* (a Chinese term that refers to the universal life force that governs well-being and personal vitality). Such treatments include Thai and aromatherapy massages, facials, body scrubs, detoxifying steam baths, and wraps.

⑤ The Oasis Spa Sukhumvit 31
MAP T6 ■ 64 Sukhumvit 31 Yaek 4 ■ 02 262 2122 ■ Open 10am–7pm daily ■ www.oasisspa.net

This day spa is set in lush tropical gardens and is tastefully decorated with teak furniture and cotton fabrics from Bali. The wide range of treatments on offer includes facials and massages, taken individually or as spa packages. Try the aloe and lavender body wrap or the Ayurvedic body massage.

6 The Grande Spa

MAP T6 ▪ The Sheraton Grande Sukhumvit, 250 Sukhumvit Road ▪ 02 649 8121 ▪ Open 10:30am–8pm daily ▪ www.sheratongrandesukhumvit.com

Located at the five-star Sheraton, this spa has an excellent reputation. Treatments combine the timeless wisdom of Thailand's healing arts with the very best of contemporary trends, and include facials, scrubs, wraps, and massages.

7 The Oasis Spa

MAP T6 ▪ 64 Sukhumvit Soi 31 ▪ 02 262 2122 ▪ Open 10am–7pm daily ▪ www.oasisspa.net

This day spa facility is set in a huge garden which helps to create an aura of calm, with birds twittering in the trees outside the treatment rooms. Options provided by the spa include an "Oasis Four Hands Massage", in which two masseurs work in unison, and the "King of Oasis", which involves massages with hot compresses and with oil.

8 Treasure Spa

MAP T6 ▪ 33 Soi 13, Soi Thonglor ▪ 02 391 7694 ▪ Open 10am–10pm daily ▪ www.treasurespa.com

This is another day spa set in a lush, tropical garden. It offers a dizzying array of treatments – massage, facial, body scrub, and body wrap, plus half-day packages. The body scrubs use tropical ingredients such

as mango and lemongrass, while the aromatherapy massage employs an aromatic blend of essential oils.

9 I. Sawan Residential Spa and Club

MAP Q3 ▪ Grand Hyatt Erawan, 494 Ratchadamri Road ▪ 02 254 6310 ▪ Open 9am–11pm daily ▪ www.hyatt.com

This luxurious spa, set amid the Grand Hyatt Erawan's lovely roof gardens, offers an extensive range of treatments, each falling into one of four categories: Energy, Harmony, Purity, or Thai.

I. Sawan Residential Spa and Club

10 Health Land

MAP N6 ▪ 120 N Sathorn Road ▪ 02 637 8883 ▪ Open 9am–10pm daily ▪ www.healthlandspa.com

This chain of spas caters to those who want a good massage and other spa services in a clean private room at a reasonable price. Full spa treatments, including facials and body polishes are on offer, and the therapists are well trained.

🔟 Sport and Leisure

T'ai chi practice at Lumphini Park

1 Martial Arts

It is possible to study and practise all kinds of martial arts in Bangkok, from Thai boxing to tae kwon do, judo, or karate, though probably the most popular is t'ai chi. To join the city's inhabitants for an impromptu session of t'ai chi or aerobics, head along to Lumphini Park *(see p86)* at dawn or dusk.

2 Horse Racing

The Royal Turf Club (RTC) in Dusit closed down, but the Royal Bangkok Sports Club (RBSC) continues to occupy a prime piece of downtown real estate. Races are held on alternate weekends at RBSC *(see p88)*. The minimum bet is an impressive B50. The Silom line of the Skytrain provides a view of the RBSC.

3 Golf

This game is very popular among visitors to Bangkok for a variety of reasons – courses are generally of a high international standard, with scenic landscaping, competitive equipment rental and green fees, and attentive and friendly service. There are several courses within easy reach of Bangkok.

4 Tennis

National Stadium: MAP N2; 154 Rama I Road; 02 214 0120
A fashionable sport in Bangkok, it is best to play early in the morning or late in the afternoon to avoid the searing heat. Major hotels have private tennis courts; public courts are at the National Stadium and in Lumphini Park *(see p86)*.

5 Takraw

Best described as volleyball played with the feet, takraw is visually exciting, with the players performing acrobatic feats to kick the ball over the net. Games are usually played early in the evening in public parks, or any small open space in Bangkok.

6 Cycling

Cycling is very popular in Bangkok. In addition to rural routes at Bang Krajao *(see p97)*, cyclists can ride in Lumphini Park *(see p86)* or on the bike lanes in the Old City. Shares and rentals are available.

7 Snooker

Since James Wattana joined the world rankings, snooker has become hugely popular in Thailand. There are thousands of clubs across the country, with hundreds of them in Bangkok. Tables are usually in excellent condition, cues are on hand, and hourly rates are reasonable.

The Royal Bangkok Sports Club golf course and race track

8 Bowling

For a fun afternoon or evening with friends, go bowling. It offers a sporting challenge without too much exertion. Most Bangkok shopping malls have a bowling alley on the top floor, some equipped with karaoke facilities and disco lighting.

9 Soccer

Thunderdome Stadium:
MAP T4; Tambon Ban Mai, Pak Kret
Although Thailand only introduced professional leagues in the mid-1990s, soccer has long been one of the country's favorite sports. Muangthong United, based at the Thunderdome Stadium, are the city's most popular team.

A Thai boxing match in progress

10 Thai Boxing

Muay Thai (Thai boxing) has enjoyed an explosion of popularity, particularly with young people, many of whom spend their holidays practising the sport in camps. Less active visitors may attend bouts at the Ratchadamnoen and Lumphini stadiums *(see p55)*.

TOP 10 THAI SPORTING EVENTS

International Kite Festival

1 Chula–Thammasat Football Match
Bangkok ▪ Jan
Held since 1934, this varsity match between two top universities features satirical parades and card stunts.

2 International Kite Festival
Hua Hin ▪ Mar
There are individual and team events at this traditional festival and a range of unusual kites are on display.

3 Chiang Mai Cricket Sixes
Chiang Mai ▪ Apr
A fun event with occasional big names.

4 Tour of Thailand
Routes vary ▪ Apr
A bicycle road race of 6 stages that draws riders from around the world.

5 Koh Samui Regatta
Chaweng Beach ▪ May/Jun
A highlight of the Asian sailing circuit.

6 Phuket Marathon
Laguna Phuket Resort ▪ Jun
Thailand's biggest marathon attracts thousands of entries each year.

7 Six Red Snooker World Championship
Bangkok ▪ Sep
Fast-paced tournament that uses six reds rather than the usual fifteen.

8 Longboat Races
Phimai & elsewhere ▪ Oct & Nov
Longboat races along town rivers.

9 Laguna Phuket Triathlon
Laguna Phuket Resort ▪ Nov
A gruelling challenge for athletes in a sport that tests their swimming, cycling, and running skills.

10 King's Cup Regatta
Phuket ▪ Dec
Since its inception in 1987, this has become Asia's premier international sailing event, and it attracts huge crowds.

🔟 **Off the Beaten Path**

① EmQuartier Tropical Garden

MAP T6 ■ Scala Building, 5th floor, EmQuartier Mall, Sukhumvit Road

No luxury goods are for sale in this part of EmQuartier mall – it's just an amazing rooftop garden with lavish displays of tropical plants, shaded resting spots, ponds, and a grassy meadow. The French designer, Patrick Blanc, added a rainforest chandelier as a finishing touch.

② Wat Hua Krabeu

MAP T2 ■ Bang Khun Tian

This Buddhist temple is the work of an eccentric monk who pays tribute to the water buffalo, Thailand's traditional draft animal, by collecting their skulls – he currently has around 10,000 of them. The temple is located on a canal, and a number of passing boats offer tours.

Buffalo skulls at Wat Hua Krabeu

③ Chao Mae Tubtim Shrine

The phallic architecture found here represents fertility and good fortune. Large stone penises stand amid the trees. Women hoping for a child come here to make offerings of incense, flowers, and wooden penises to the resident spirit. This is a peaceful spot *(see p88)* by the Saen Saeb canal.

④ Chinatown's Soi Nana

MAP F5 ■ Between Charoen Krung and Luang roads, Chinatown

Not to be confused with the go-go-bar area of the same name on Sukhumvit Road, this residential neighborhood buzzes with chic cafés, art galleries, bars with live music, and small restaurants. Try the Tep Bar *(see p81)* for innovative tunes and Thai food.

⑤ Sathorn Road, Sois 10–12

MAP M6

A range of cuisines can be found in this cluster of chic independent restaurants and cafés on a tree-lined loop off Sathorn Road. With several lively nightspots *(see p92)* located nearby, it's very popular with young professionals, both Thai and from the expat community.

⑥ Queen Sirikit Museum of Textiles

Often overlooked by visitors to the Grand Palace, as it is situated on the right just after the main entrance, this superb museum *(see pp12–13)* displays a fine collection of textiles from throughout Asia, with an emphasis on the royal attire and the renowned and luxurious Thai silk. The grand building (formerly the Royal Treasury) gleams with white marble from Italy.

Exhibits at the Bangkokian Museum

⑦ Bangkokian Museum

MAP M5 ▪ 273 Saphan Yao Alley, Si Phraya ▪ 02 233 7027 ▪ Open 9am–4pm Tue–Sun ▪ Adm

This gorgeous World War II-era museum provides an insight into mid-20th century life in Bangkok. The property, once home to a wealthy Bangkok family, displays the family's possessions, including period crockery, furniture, and a rudimentary television.

⑧ Bang Krajao

Often called Bangkok's green lung, this protected enclave (see p97) is on the west bank of the Chao Phraya River and is easy to reach by boat (from behind Wat Klong Toey Nok, among other piers). It's an ideal spot for cycling, with bikes available for rent, and there is also a market here on weekends. The area is also gaining a reputation for its popular eco-resort (see p117).

⑨ Museum of Forensic Medicine

MAP A3 ▪ Siriraj Hospital, Thonburi ▪ 02 419 2601 ▪ Open 10am–5pm Wed–Mon ▪ Adm ▪ www.siriraj museum.com

Its local nickname, "Museum of Death," sums up this fascinating place. Skeletons, embalmed bodies (including the remains of a notorious serial killer), and crime-scene evidence all make for a grisly yet informative visit. Other museums exploring medicine and local history can also be found on the hospital's grounds and are worth checking out while here.

Traditional Chinese medicine on display at the Museum of Forensic Medicine

⑩ Friese-Greene Cinema

MAP T6 ▪ 259/6 Sukhumvit Road, Khlong Tan ▪ www.fgc.in.th

Named after the motion picture pioneer William Friese-Greene, this cinema hosts screenings of classic, cult, and indie films. It is technically a member's club, but a visit is worth the nominal yearly fee. It also has a vast library of cinema-related books.

Cycleway over the river in the green surroundings of Bang Krajao

Children's Attractions

Roller coaster soaring over Dream World amusement park

1 Dream World

MAP T2 ▪ 62 Moo 1, Rangsit-Nakornnayok Road, Thanyaburi, Pathumthani ▪ 02 577 8666 ▪ Open 10am–5pm daily ▪ Adm ▪ www.dreamworld.co.th

Featuring a hanging roller coaster, a sightseeing train, water rides and various other amusements, the Dream World theme park comprises different areas, including Snow Town, Fantasy Land as well as a haunted mansion.

2 Siam Amazing Park

MAP U5 ▪ 203 Suan Sayam Road, Khan Na Yao ▪ 02 105 4294 ▪ Open 10am–6pm daily ▪ Adm ▪ www.siamamazingpark.com

The first amusement and water park in Southeast Asia has been providing fun for families since 1980. Highlights include rollercoasters, a log flume, and a pirate ship ride. The park also features a thrilling animatronic dinosaur adventure area.

Children playing inside Harbor Land

3 The Queen Saovabha Memorial Institute

Founded as the Pasteur Institute in 1923, the Queen Saovabha Memorial Institute (see p85), named after one of Rama V's wives, is now run by the Red Cross. Shows to educate the public about the dangers of Thai snakes are held here every day (11am & 2pm Mon–Fri, 11am Sat & Sun)

4 Harbor Land

MAP U5 ▪ Floor 3, Fashion Island Mall, Khan Na Yao ▪ Open 10am–8pm daily ▪ Adm ▪ www.harborlandgroup.com

Popular with children, this colorful activity center in the Fashion Island mall has fun slides, ball pits, and play areas. It also offers trike racing tracks, and trampolines.

5 Pororo Aqua Park

MAP U6 ▪ 6th Floor, Central Plaza Bangna, 587–9 Debaratana Road ▪ 02 0745 7377 ▪ Open 10am–7pm daily ▪ Adm ▪ www.pororoaquapark.com

Kids and adults of all ages will love the slides, pools, and rides at this water park, located to the east of Bangkok. Shallow pools provide a safe space for smaller children to play in, while winding corkscrew slides provide plenty of fun for older children.

6 Bangkok Butterfly Garden and Insectarium

MAP T5 ■ Suan Vachirabenchathat (Rotfai or Railway Park), Kamphaeng Phet 3 Road ■ 02 272 4359 ■ Open 8:30am–4:30pm Tue–Sun

Walking distance from Chatuchak Park subway station and Mo Chit Skytrain station, this park *(see p63)* is home to over 500 butterflies. There is a study center and a children's playground on site. Visitors can rent bikes in the adjacent park, which has family-oriented cycle routes.

Exhibit at Bangkok Dolls Museum

7 Bangkok Dolls Museum

This museum *(see p98)* was created by Tongkorn Chandavimol in the 1950s after a visit to Japan, which aroused her interest in dolls from different countries and eras, which are dressed in miniature costumes and presented in context. The dolls here, from her own collection, are from all over the world. Handcrafted dolls can be bought in the adjacent workshop for B500.

Beautifully shaded Lumphini Park

8 Lumphini Park

Named after the birthplace of the Buddha in Nepal, this is the only decent-sized park *(see p86)* in the center of Bangkok. It has lots of shady trees and a large lake.

9 Children's Discovery Museum

MAP T5 ■ Queen Sirikit Park, Kamphaengphet Road ■ 02 246 6144 ■ Open 10am–4pm Tue–Sun

Hands-on exhibits include a Science Discovery Zone, and Incredible Me, where children can learn about their bodies, senses, and emotions.

10 Flow House

MAP T6 ■ A-Square, 120/1 Sukhumvit Soi 26 ■ 02 108 5210 ■ Open 11am–9pm Tue–Sun ■ Adm (no children under 5) ■ www.flowhousethailand.com

The wave-simulating surfing machine here is guaranteed to pacify the most restless of adolescents. There is a bit of a learning curve involved, so instructors are always on hand.

Following pages Panoramic view of the cityscape over Lumphini Park

TOP 10 Entertainment Venues

A stage full of actors and dancers at the National Theatre

1 National Theatre
MAP B3 ■ Rachini Road
■ 02 224 1342 ■ Adm

Productions of Thai classical drama such as *khon* (masked theater) with actors in sumptuous costumes are staged twice a month, on Sundays, at the National Theatre. An impressive medley of dances and musical shows are also performed here.

2 Muangthai Rachadalai Theatre
MAP T5 ■ Ratchadaphisek Road
■ 02 224 1342 ■ Adm ■ www.
rachadalai.com

Claiming to be "Thailand's first Broadway-standard theater", this institution hosts touring productions and musical and dance shows that outline the history and culture of Thailand.

3 Living Room
One of Bangkok's finest jazz venues *(see p101)*, Living Room is a cozy and stylishly adorned spot in the slick Sheraton Grande hotel. The jazz shows held here feature local and international performances, and are accompanied by a variety of good food, including afternoon tea and traditional Thai dishes.

4 Tawandang German Brewery
Enjoy a wildly entertaining cabaret, featuring Thai as well as Western pop and folk music, ballet, hip-hop dancing, and magic shows at the Tawandang German Brewery *(see p101)*. The huge dome of this vast all-round venue can host up to 1,600 revellers and it offers good food and great micro-brewed German beer.

5 Sala Chalermkrung Royal Theatre
MAP C5 ■ Charoen Krung Road ■ 02 224 4499 ■ Khon: 7:30pm Fri ■ Adm
■ www.salachalermkrung.com

Built in 1933 by Rama VII, this was Thailand's first theater to be built with the intention of screening "talking pictures." Today this theater is used for staging *khon* (masked theater) and for entertaining live performances by skilled singers and musicians.

Inside Muangthai Rachadalai Theatre

6 Thailand Cultural Centre

MAP T5 ■ Ratchadaphisek Road
■ 02 247 0028 ■ www.culture.go.th

Bangkok's main center for the performing arts, this state-run facility is home to the Bangkok Symphony Orchestra. It also hosts the annual International Festival of Dance and Music *(see p64)*. International artists also perform here during world tours, so check for upcoming events.

7 Ratchadamnoen Boxing Stadium

MAP E2 ■ 1 Ratchadamnoen Nok Road ■ 02 281 4205 ■ Bouts: 6:30–11pm Mon, Wed & Thu; 5–8pm & 8:30pm–midnight Sun ■ Adm

Infused with the philosophy and elegance of martial arts, Thai boxing, or *muay Thai*, is a thrilling sport to watch. The chance to see the excitement of "the art of eight limbs" up close is an unforgettable part of a trip to Bangkok, with the fighters' traditional clothing and pre-match music adding to the sense of high theater.

8 Calypso Cabaret

Bangkok's famous cabaret show is not only a riot of sequins, song and dance, but also an insight into Thailand's LGBTQ+ community, which has long been a visible part of society here. During the nightly performances, transgender artists lip-sync to iconic show tunes and popular Chinese, Japanese, and Korean songs. Tickets can include dinner at the Calypso Thai Restaurant, located within the same building as the performance theater.

9 Sala Rim Naam

MAP M5 ■ Mandarin Oriental Hotel ■ 02 659 9000 ■ Lunch: noon–2:30pm daily; dinner: 7–10:30pm daily; show: 7:45pm daily ■ www.mandarinoriental.com

This is a custom-built facility offering a show of traditional Thai dance and a gourmet dinner. Prices are above average, but the event is memorable.

The dining area at Sala Rim Naam

10 Lumphini Boxing Stadium

In 2014, this stadium *(see p101)* moved out to the northern suburbs. Slightly more prestigious than Ratchadamnoen Stadium, Lumphini hosts top Thai boxing fights on Tuesdays and Fridays. Check website for upcoming fights.

A performer at Calypso Cabaret

🔟 Bars and Clubs

Live music at Adhere the 13th

1 Adhere the 13th (Blues Bar)

This tiny hole-in-the-wall bar *(see p74)*, popularly known as the Blues Bar, has a welcoming atmosphere, sociable pavement seats, and well-priced beer and cocktails. The Thai and expat bands play mostly blues and jazz, with special weekend events proving to be the big crowd-pullers.

2 Sky Bar

Famous for alfresco drinks, this standing-only bar *(see p92)* featured in *The Hangover II*. It is built 902-ft (275-m) above the city's pavements, with almost 360-degree views. Come early to enjoy the stunning panoramas as the sun sets.

3 Saxophone

The music here *(see p93)* is impressive with three sets every night, mixing jazz and acoustic with blues, rock, and reggae. Prices are moderate.

4 The Club@Koi

Attached to a Californian-style Japanese restaurant, Bangkok's coolest nightclub *(see p93)* pulls in a dress-to-impress crowd, with music varying by the night. There are booths, standing tables, a dance floor, and great views of the city from its 39th-floor Lounge.

5 Bamboo Bar

With its relaxed atmosphere and great lineups, this is a fantastic spot *(see p93)* to unwind and listen to smooth jazz. It has an elegant atmosphere, and the attentive staff ensure they keep the drinks flowing.

6 Maggie Choo's

Discreet and opulent, the prohibition era of 1930s Shanghai has been recreated in this trendy bar *(see p93)*. Leather armchairs and couches are surrounded by Art Deco lamps and Khmer statues, and the brick walls are original – it was once a bank vault. There's live jazz later in the evenings and good food.

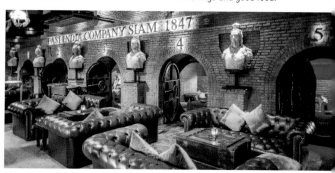

Shanghai prohibition-era decadence at Maggie Choo's

7 Levels

Each of the three party zones *(see p93)* at this famous nightspot has its own atmosphere and vibe, from raucous house to sophisticated lounge music. Check out all three to experience the full effect.

8 Brown Sugar: The Jazz Boutique

This long-established jazz bar *(see p74)* is one of Bangkok's iconic night-time venues. Being the city's premier jazz venue it attracts some exceptionally talented musicians. It features a nightly acoustic set followed by bands. There's an extra midnight set on Friday and Saturday, and a jam session on Sunday.

Musician playing at Brown Sugar

9 Studio Lam

This small bar *(see p100)* is run by the DJs of Zudrangma Records, who play *morlam,* folk music from northeastern Thailand, and an eclectic choice of beats from around the world on a massive, purpose-built sound system.

10 Hyde and Seek

A sophisticated gastropub, Hyde and Seek *(see p92)* serves imported draught beers. It also offers a wide selection of wines by the glass, as well as good bar bites, pastas, and comfort food.

TOP 10 LGBTQ+ BARS AND CLUBS

Gay bars in the Soi Twilight district

1 The Balcony
MAP P5 ▪ Silom Soi 4
At the heart of Bangkok's LGBTQ+ scene, the Balcony bar offers cheap food and great value evening happy hours.

2 The Stranger Bar
MAP P5 ▪ Silom Soi 4
This bar features drag shows every night, and serves great cocktails.

3 Disco Disco
MAP P5 ▪ Silom Soi 2
This bar-meets-disco is one of the top places to see and be seen in Bangkok.

4 DJ Station
A popular gay disco *(see p93)* that is packed to the rafters almost every night.

5 The Expresso
MAP P5 ▪ Silom Soi 4
This bar is a good place to chill out and take in the action in Soi 2.

6 Jupiter 2018
MAP P5 ▪ Silom Soi 4
Enjoy the live dance show at Jupiter 2018, a popular gay go-go bar.

7 G Bangkok
MAP P5 ▪ Silom Road (between Soi 2 and Soi 4)
This late-night club fills up even after the DJ Station closes.

8 Telephone Pub
MAP P5 ▪ 114/11–13 Silom Soi 4
This pub is named for the phones that once offered table-to-table contact.

9 Fork and Cork
MAP P5 ▪ 104 Silom Soi 4
The good range of food served at this bar appeals to a classy crowd.

10 BAS Living Room
MAP P5 ▪ 114/5 Silom 4 Alley
A chilled-out option in this lively locale, with good deals for drinks.

🔟 Restaurants

Lavish interior at Le Normandie, with calming river views

① Le Normandie

An institution in the venerable Oriental Hotel, Le Normandie *(see p91)* serves classic French food and has a relaxing ambience, lavish decor, views on the river, and impeccable service. Specialties include duck foie gras and Brittany lobster, and the wine list offers over 200 French wines.

② Bo.Lan

MAP T6 ▪ 24 Sukhumvit Soi 53 ▪ 02 260 2962 ▪ Opening times vary, call ahead

Thai food at its finest is served at this legendary Bangkok restaurant, which now operates as a shop for artisan products as well as a venue for cooking workshops and regular dining experiences. Expect eclectic yet classic Thai cuisine made from the freshest organic ingredients.

Thai fine-dining at Bo.Lan

③ Goji Kitchen and Bar

Located in the rarefied environs of the Marriott Marquis Queen's Park, this modern restaurant *(see p91)* offers succulent barbecued meat, fresh sushi, and rich noodle dishes – all exhibiting a committed farm-to-table philosophy.

④ Blue Elephant

Located in a European-style mansion, the Blue Elephant *(see p99)* offers a menu of Royal Thai cuisine, ranging from classic staples to experimental creations. There are many tasty starters on offer, and the salmon larb main is highly recommended. There's also a jazzy cocktail bar.

⑤ Issaya Siamese Club

Delicious Thai food with a contemporary twist is served in a 1920s mansion *(see p91)* with private dining rooms. There's bright, quirky furnishings and a garden outside. The chef's choices are indicated on the menu, including *yam hua plii* (banana flower salad with crunchy dressing) and lamb shank *massaman* curry.

⑥ Lenzi Tuscan Kitchen

Choosing the best Italian in Bangkok is hard, but Lenzi *(see p91)* is a strong contender. The chef, formerly of the excellent Opus Wine Bar, has perfectly re-created the cuisine of his native Tuscany. The food and the service are excellent.

7 Eat Me

This art gallery and restaurant *(see p91)* has changing exhibitions on the walls and alfresco seating on the covered balconies. The truffle and Parmesan risotto and pappardelle with rabbit *ragù* are among the many international specialties here. The desserts are excellent, too.

8 Liu

A standout among Bangkok's Chinese restaurants, this place *(see p91)* is becoming famous for its Peking duck. The *dong po* (stewed pork belly and black soy sauce served with Chinese buns), is also excellent. The atmosphere is quiet and elegant.

9 Rang Mahal

Often named by Indians as the best Indian food in the city, Rang Mahal *(see p91)* has been perfecting its fare for more than 20 years. There's live but discreet Indian music in the evenings. The views from its 26th-floor perch atop the Rembrandt Hotel are incredible.

10 Gaggan

Consistently voted among the world's top 50 in *Restaurant* magazine, Gaggan *(see p91)* makes progressive Indian food using molecular gastronomy techniques. With a relaxed ambience in a converted wooden house, it has panache in both menu and service.

Relaxed dining area at Gaggan

TOP 10 CULINARY HIGHLIGHTS

Bowl of *tom yam kung*

1 Tom Yam Kung
Thailand's signature dish – a hot and spicy soup with chilies, lemongrass, and galangal – is typically served with prawns or seafood.

2 Phat Thai
Literally "Thai fry," this delicious noodle dish with beansprouts, peanuts, and eggs is a great lunchtime filler.

3 Kaeng Phanaeng
This thick curry made with coconut cream and spices is usually served with pork or chicken, plus a side of rice.

4 Nam Prik Num
This delicious, gooey dip made of pounded chilies and eggplant seems to typify Thai cuisine with its spicy taste and creamy texture.

5 Sticky Rice
Thais from the north and northeast of the country often press a ball of sticky rice into their dips and sauces.

6 Som Tam
Unripe (green) papaya is shredded finely and mixed with dried shrimp, lemon juice, tomatoes, peanuts, fish sauce, and chilies to make this salad.

7 Phat Pak Bung
Morning glory, one of Thailand's tastiest green vegetables, is fried with garlic and chilis in oyster sauce for this crunchy, nutritious dish.

8 Mango with Sticky Rice
A delicious dessert of ripe mango with sticky rice and a coconut milk sauce.

9 Coconut Custard
This dessert is a sweet concoction of coconut milk, eggs, and sugar.

10 Fruit Juices and Shakes
Most Thai fruits can be served as tasty, thirst-quenching juices, or shakes when mixed with yoghurt.

🔟 Markets and Shopping

Entrance to Asiatique the Riverfront

1 Asiatique the Riverfront

MAP S6 ▪ Charoen Krung Road, between Soi 72 and Soi 76 ▪ Open 4pm–midnight Mon–Fri, noon–midnight Sat & Sun ▪ www.asiatique thailand.com

This open-air night market and entertainment zone has hundreds of cool boutiques, restaurants, the cabaret show Calypso (see p101), and a huge Ferris wheel. Despite being touristy, it's well done and good fun.

2 Siam Paragon

This mall (see p89) connects with its two adjacent neighbours, Siam Center and Siam Discovery. While the featured items are mainly international luxury brands, there are also clothing and accessories from top Thai designers. All three offer a plethora of designer clothes, restaurants, cinemas, and book and music shops.

3 Mahboonkrong Shopping Center

While most of Bangkok's shopping malls have a clinical, international feel to them, Mahboonkrong (see p89) feels more local. Also known as MBK, this mall sprawls across seven floors. It is packed with stalls selling souvenirs and cheap clothes. There are also bigger outlets selling jewelry and a branch of the Japanese Tokyu Department Store.

4 Central World

Bangkok's largest mall (see p89), accessible by Skywalk from Siam Paragon, has everything from designer items to funky boutiques, bookstores, and electronic equipment in more than 500 stores. There are also some excellent restaurants, 15 cinemas, a kids' zone, and an ice-skating rink within the complex.

5 Pratunam

Leaving Central World, a Skywalk leads to the Pratunam area (see p88), where things move downmarket a bit. Cluttering the sidewalk and spilling over into several small lanes, this bustling market is great for cheap clothes, as well as luggage, gadgets, souvenirs, and more. Platinum Fashion Mall nearby is a large air-conditioned version of Pratunam.

Siam Paragon

6 Emporium and EmQuartier

These neighboring malls (see p89) cover both sides of Sukhumvit Road, joined by a Skywalk. While the Emporium is dedicated to high fashion and some fine restaurants, the newer EmQuartier is more diverse and boutique-oriented. It also has a really lovely garden (see p48).

7 Lalai Sap Market

MAP P5 ■ Soi 5 (Soi Surasena), Silom Road ■ Open 8am–4pm Mon–Fri

For a look at a vibrant, traditional Bangkokian street market – away from the more luxurious tourist equivalents – head to Lalai Sap. There are small restaurants (busy with office workers at noon) and stalls selling inexpensive clothing and accessories. The market's name means "Money Melts," but it melts in small denominations here.

8 Terminal 21

MAP T6 ■ Sukhumvit Road, corner of Soi 21 (Asok Montri Road) ■ 02 108 0888 ■ Open 10am–10pm daily ■ www.terminal21.co.th

This huge mall resembles a futuristic airport terminal, and each of the nine floors is decorated in city themes, from San Francisco to Rome. Mid-range clothing and boutiques abound, as do good restaurants. The relaxed atmosphere here tends to attract a younger and more local clientele than many of the other Sukhumvit malls.

9 Pantip Plaza

MAP Q2 ■ New Phetburi Road ■ 02 250 1555 ■ Open 10am–10pm daily ■ www.pantipplaza.com

This IT mecca sells the latest computer programs as well as digital cameras and other electronics. Although it is crammed with hardware and software, the mall is rife with counterfeit products. Despite regular police raids, vendors dealing in pirated goods stay in business thanks to their customers' huge appetite for such stuff.

Clothes at Sampeng Lane Market

10 Sampeng Lane Market

The market held on this narrow street is lined with shops selling household goods, fashion accessories, shoes, and clothing. Phahurat Road (see p77) leads into Sampeng Lane (see p78), and walking from one to the other feels like hopping from India to China.

🔟 Bangkok for Free

1 Visit Temples

Most temples in Bangkok, such as Wat Mahathat and Wat Ratchabophit *(see p72)*, are free to enter and offer a pleasant respite from the clamor of the city. All that is required is respectful dress and a quiet demeanor. Remove your shoes at the entrance of the largest building, sit for a while, and absorb the calming atmosphere.

Wat Ratchabophit's entrance

2 Thai Boxing at MBK Shopping Center

MAP P3 ▪ Corner of Phaya Thai and Rama I roads ▪ 02 620 9000 ▪ Bouts 6pm Wednesday

Traditional *muay Thai* matches *(see p47)* are held outside Tokyu Department Store and run into the evening. These are not the watered-down exhibition matches held at tourist venues – the crowd is raucous and the punches and kicks are real.

3 Puppet Show at Artist's House in Khlong Bang Luang

MAP S6 ▪ Soi Wat Thong Sala Ngarm, Thonburi ▪ 02 868 5279 ▪ Performances 2pm Wed & Fri–Sun

On the Thonburi side of the river, this place is a bit hard to find but worth the effort. A project by a local artist here keeps Thai culture alive with traditional Thai puppet shows. There are also free art exhibits and a coffee shop.

4 Phra Athit Park Aerobics

MAP C2 ▪ Phra Athit Road

Next to the Prom Phra Sumen Fort, on the Chao Phraya River, this small but beautiful park hosts informal aerobics classes starting an hour before sunset every day. A leader on stage shows the movements and gives encouragement to all the exercisers taking part.

5 Bangkok Art & Culture Centre

An oasis of calm amid the malls in Bangkok's prime shopping zone, the BACC *(see p43)* is a striking, white contemporary art museum that always has a wide choice of exhibitions and events on. There's usually an interesting exhibition on here, as well as a performance in one of the performance spaces.

6 Thai Dancing at Erawan Shrine

This holy shrine *(see p86)* in Bangkok's shopping district venerates the Hindu God Brahma. Thais come to make offerings of flowers and incense. They also commission the resident Thai classical dancers to perform for the spirits.

Thai dancers at Erawan Shrine

T'ai chi practitioners in Lumphini Park

7 Lumphini Park T'ai Chi

As soon as dawn breaks, aficionados of this ancient Chinese dance-like practice start their routines *(see p86)*. Visitors are always very welcome to participate: simply stand at the back of the group and follow the movements.

8 Bangkok Butterfly Garden

A respite from the nearby weekend market, this park *(see p51)* within a park has open areas where the butterflies live, as well as displays of various specimens under glass.

Bangkok Butterfly Garden

9 Neilson Hays Library Art Galleries

MAP N5 ■ 195 Surawong Road ■ 02 233 1731 ■ Open 9:30am–5pm Tue–Sun ■ www.neilsonhayslibrary.org

Housed in a beautiful Neo-Classical building, the private Neilson Hays Library has two excellent art galleries: the Rotunda and the Garden Café.

10 Meditation Course at Wat Mahathat

Introductory walk-in courses in Buddhist meditation start at 7am, 1pm, and 6pm and cover both seated and walking techniques. A brief lecture introduces the three-hour session. The temple *(see p72)* also offers longer residential courses, with food and accommodation provided; a donation is usually expected for these courses.

TOP 10 BUDGET TIPS

1 Get a local SIM card for your phone. Kiosks offer short-term plans at the airport and in all city malls. Data speeds are very good in Bangkok.

2 If you make any significant purchases, you can get a refund of the 7 per cent VAT when leaving Thailand.

3 Bangkok's mass transit systems – the MRT, BTS Skytrain, and Airport Rail Link – cover most of the city.

4 The Chao Phraya Express Boat Service is a great way to see all the river sights and beat the traffic.

5 *Bangkok 101* and *The Big Chilli* are great magazines (and websites) that feature free events and promotions in the city. *BK* magazine and its website is more listings-driven, but is free.

6 Guesthouses such as the A-One Inn *(see p116)* are clean and cheap.

7 Bargaining is perfectly appropriate for any non-food item in a street market. Offer 50 per cent and keep on smiling.

8 Imported alcoholic drinks are taxed up to 400 per cent here, but the local beers (such as Singha, Leo, and Chang) are good, as is the rum – try Sang Som with soda and a squeeze of lime.

9 Traditional massage venues do not offer the luxury that you will find in the spas, but these ubiquitous shops offer good body or foot massages at very reasonable prices.

10 All shopping malls have air-conditioned food courts, often in the basement, where a variety of vendors offer local specialties for much less than you would pay in restaurants.

Food court of Siam Paragon

Festivals

Revellers watching the colorful lion dance during Chinese New Year

① Chinese New Year
Chinatown ▪ **Jan or Feb**

This week-long Thai-Chinese celebration has lion dances in the street, lots of loud firecrackers, and colorful activities in temples.

② Makha Puja
Citywide ▪ **Feb or Mar**

This annual Buddhist festival, held at the full moon, celebrates the Buddha's first sermon to 1,250 disciples, starting the dissemination of the *dhamma*.

Monks observing Makha Puja

③ Songkran
Citywide ▪ **Mid–Apr**

Thai New Year is the country's most chaotic and raucous festival. People throw water over each other as a symbolic form of cleansing to usher in the new year, and passers-by are not spared. Perhaps for its novelty value, this festival is particularly popular among foreign visitors.

④ Royal Ploughing Ceremony
Sanam Luang ▪ **Early May**

This annual event is designed to give an auspicious start to the new planting season. Sacred white oxen are used to plough a ritual field in Sanam Luang *(see p69)* near the Grand Palace *(see pp12–13)*, which is then sown with rice seeds blessed by the king. Farmers rush to collect the seeds to plant in their own fields.

⑤ Visakha Puja
Citywide ▪ **May**

The holiest day of the Buddhist calendar commemorates the Buddha's birth, enlightenment, and death. Occurring on the day of the full-moon, the evening candlelit procession around the temple is notable, especially at Wat Benjamabophit *(see p40)*.

⑥ International Festival of Dance and Music
Thailand Cultural Centre ▪ **Sep & Oct**

Since 1999, Bangkok's premier international arts festival has been held at the Thailand Cultural Centre *(see p55)* in September and October each year. It features acts from around the world, along with some of Thailand's best performers. The focus of the festival is mainly on opera, ballet, and classical music, though jazz and modern dance are represented as well.

7 Loy Krathong
Citywide ■ Nov

This festival, usually held in November, offers homage to the goddess of the waters for providing a successful harvest. Beautiful *krathong* (small decorated floats) are released onto the river at night while fireworks light up the sky.

8 Wat Saket Fair
Golden Mount ■ Nov

Temple fairs in Thailand are like village fêtes in the West, and this one at Wat Saket and the Golden Mount (see p70), held just before or after Loy Krathong, is a good example. It has a great atmosphere, with music, theater and lots of kids having fun.

Performers at Wat Saket fair

9 Cat Expo
Wonderworld Fun Park ■ Nov

Formerly known as Fat Festival, this is Thailand's biggest Indie music event that features more than a hundred established as well as emerging bands. There are booths where you can meet the bands, and watch films.

10 King Bhumibol's Birthday
Citywide ■ Dec

Celebrated on December 5, this is both a national holiday and Fathers' Day, Thais have long celebrated the birthday of Rama IX, who died in late 2016. It's possible that this will remain on the calendar, with the new king Vajiralongkorn's birthday on July 28 added as a further holiday.

TOP 10 UP-COUNTRY FESTIVALS

Chiang Mai Flower Festival parade

1 Chiang Mai Flower Festival
First weekend, Feb
A parade of marching bands precedes floats bedecked with flowers.

2 ASEAN Barred Ground Dove Festival
First week, Mar
This dove-singing contest attracts competitors from far and wide to Yala.

3 Pattaya Music Festival
Mar
Thai musicians and international acts play in a wide variety of styles.

4 Poy Sang Long
First weekend, Apr
A Shan festival held in Chiang Mai and Mae Hong Son in which ordaining novices are paraded round the streets.

5 Rocket Festival
May
In the northeast, especially Yasothon, home-made rockets are fired to trigger the start of the monsoons.

6 Hua Hin Jazz Festival
May
This beach festival attracts big names.

7 Phi Ta Khon
Jun/Jul
Locals in Dan Sai dress as spirits for this wild and colorful event in Loei province.

8 Phuket Vegetarian Festival
Oct
Acts of self-mortification draw in the crowds for nine days.

9 Lanna Boat Races
Oct/Nov
At the end of the Buddhist Lent; the most exciting are in Nan Province.

10 Elephant Round-Up
Nov
Surin, in the northeast, is the venue for this pachyderm extravaganza.

Bangkok
Area by Area

The modern, glittering skyline
of Bangkok after dark

🔟 Old City

Bangkok's historical heart lies in the Old City. When Chao Phraya Chakri, later pronounced Rama I, assumed the throne in 1782,

he had a canal dug across a neck of land on the east bank of the Chao Phraya River to create an island that emulated the former capital at Ayutthaya. This island became known as Rattanakosin; now, it and the area to its east are known as the Old City. Here stand the Grand Palace, once home of the royal family, and Wat Phra Kaeo, a glittering temple that houses the Emerald Buddha, as well as several important temples, museums, universities, and Sanam Luang.

Wheel from royal funeral chariot

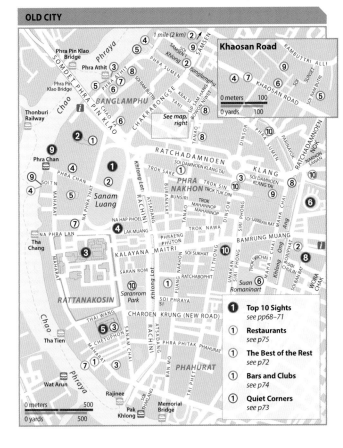

OLD CITY

Khaosan Road

	Top 10 Sights see pp68–71
1	**Restaurants** see p75
1	**The Best of the Rest** see p72
1	**Bars and Clubs** see p74
1	**Quiet Corners** see p73

1 Sanam Luang
MAP B3 ▪ Na Phra Lan Road

Considering Bangkok's congested streets and high-rise buildings, it is amazing that a large open area such as Sanam Luang, or Royal Field, could exist at all. Its importance for certain royal ceremonies, such as cremation rites of royalty, guarantee that this precious patch of land will never be developed into offices or malls. From February to April, people fly kites here, and fortune tellers ply their trade.

2 National Museum

Located near the northern end of Rattanakosin Island, the National Museum *(see pp16–17)* is the repository of significant Thai art. Its huge size reflects the depth of Thai artistic achievement. Exhibits range from Dvaravati sculptures over 1,000 years old, to lavish funeral chariots, and the delightful Buddhaisawan Chapel, which houses the Phra Sihing Buddha image, considered second in importance only to the Emerald Buddha in Wat Phra Kaeo.

3 Grand Palace and Wat Phra Kaeo

In the center of Rattanakosin Island, the huge complex that contains the Grand Palace and Wat Phra Kaeo *(see pp12–15)* is one of Asia's unforgettable sights. It is the best place for an introduction to Thai architecture and art. While the palace is strongly influenced by Italian Renaissance architecture, the temple complex is unmistakably Thai, from the towering *bot* (ordination hall) that holds the Emerald Buddha to the slender lines of the Phra Si Rattana Chedi and the *Ramakien* murals that decorate the galleries on all sides.

Majestic facade of Wat Phra Kaeo

4 Lak Muang
MAP C4 ▪ Corner of Ratchadamnoen and Lak Muang roads ▪ Open 8:30am–5:30pm daily

This shrine houses the city pillar of Bangkok, erected by Rama I in 1782 and believed to contain the city's guardian spirit, Jao Pho Lak Muang. Also in the shrine is the city pillar of Thonburi, now part of Greater Bangkok. Both pillars are made of wood with lotus-shaped crowns and are painted gold. Lak Muang is always busy with devotees.

City pillars at Lak Muang

5 Wat Pho

Officially Wat Phra Chetuphon, this *(see pp18–19)* is Bangkok's oldest and largest temple and a welcoming center of learning, particularly of the massage techniques for which it is famous. While Wat Phra Kaeo impresses with bejeweled monuments, Wat Pho's charms are more subtle. The main attraction is the 150-ft (46-m) long Reclining Buddha that fills a *wihan* (assembly hall) in the compound's northwest corner, but it can be just as much fun exploring quieter corners of the grounds and chatting with the monks, schoolchildren, and massage practitioners.

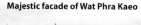

6 Wat Saket and the Golden Mount

Wat Saket: MAP E3 ▪ Golden Mount: MAP D3; 344 Chakkaphatdi Phong Road; 02 621 2280; open 7:30am–7pm daily; adm (for Golden Mount)

This was one of the first temples built when the city was founded in the late 1700s, initially as a crematorium for the common people. Fine murals adorn the walls of the *wihan* (assembly hall). Climb the 320 steps to the summit of the Golden Mount, a 250-ft (76-m) high artificial hill surmounted by a graceful golden, bell-shaped *chedi* (stupa), for fine views of the Old City skyline.

Bowls being made at Soi Ban Baat

SPIRITS IN THAI SOCIETY

Lak Muang, the Amulet Market, and spirit houses (shrines dedicated to the spirit of the land on which a house is built) are all animist manifestations, which demonstrate that Thai religious belief is not limited to Buddhism. In fact, Buddhism's prevalence here is partly due to its assimilation of aspects of other belief systems, such as Hinduism.

7 River and Canal Tour

Many visitors to Bangkok want to take a trip on the river and nearby canals *(see pp20–21)* to get a sense of how the city was before the motor car and catch a glimpse of traditional canal-side life. There are many tours that may be organized via your hotel or guesthouse. Alternatively, negotiate a price with a longtail-boat owner at any of the principal piers, and arrange a customized tour.

8 Soi Ban Baat

MAP D4 ▪ Soi Ban Baat, Boriphat Road

Buddhist monks have few material possessions – the *baat* (alms bowl) is one of them. Early each morning the bowls are filled with food offerings by devout Buddhists. They are mostly made in factories, but in Soi Ban Baat, or Monk's Bowl Village, there are still a few families that beat out the bowls by hand. Traditionally, these *baat* are made of eight strips of metal to represent the Eightfold Path of Buddhism. First, they are welded in a kiln, then shaped and filed smooth, and finally fired again.

9 Amulet Market

MAP B4 ▪ Maharat Road and small lanes ▪ Open 8am–6pm daily

There is a strong belief among Thais that small images of the

Boating down a canal

Buddha, famous kings, or even tigers' teeth worn as pendants can provide protection from misfortune. It is, therefore, quite common to see people wearing a string of such amulets around the neck, and some even become ardent collectors of amulets. One of the best places to see this faith demonstrated is in the Amulet Market on the streets around Wat Mahathat, where potential buyers will carefully scrutinize the tiny objects with magnifying glasses and quiz the vendor to ascertain the amulet's properties.

Traditional art at Wat Suthat

⑩ Wat Suthat
MAP D4 ▪ 146 Bamrung Muang Road ▪ 02 224 9845 ▪ Open 9am–4pm daily ▪ Adm

Begun in 1807 by Rama I (r.1782–1807) and completed by his successors, Wat Suthat is one of Bangkok's most important temples. Fronted by the towering Sao Ching Cha, a giant swing that was once used for a Brahmin ceremony, the compound has the tallest *wihan* in the city, especially constructed to accommodate the Phra Sri Sakyamuni Buddha, a 26-ft (8-m) tall 14th-century Sukhothai image. The murals in the *wihan* are beautifully detailed, and the temple grounds include four lovely bronze horses.

A STROLL THROUGH THE OLD CITY

Amulet Market
Sanam Luang
Bamrung Muang Road
Wat Saket, Golden Mount
S&P Restaurant
Krua Apsorn
Lak Muang
Maharat Rd
Silpakorn University Art Exhibition Hall
Sanam Chai Rd
Wat Suthat
Sao Ching Cha
Soi Ban Baat
Wat Phra Kaeo

▶ MORNING

Begin your exploration of the Old City at **Wat Saket**, where you can climb the **Golden Mount** to enjoy a wonderful, panoramic view of the area. From here walk south along Boriphat Road until you reach **Soi Ban Baat**, where alms bowls are beaten out of strips of metal. Go back up Boriphat Road, then left into **Bamrung Muang Road** *(see p72)* where shops sell Buddha images and temple paraphernalia. When you reach the unmissable giant swing known as Sao Ching Cha, turn into **Wat Suthat** and appreciate the superb carvings and paintings on display. Go over the canal and turn right onto Sanam Chai Road for the lush green lawns of **Sanam Luang** *(see p69)*. For lunch, head north up Dinsor Road and join the civil servants at **Krua Apsorn** *(see p75)*, tuck into fiery and traditional central Thai dishes such as green curry with fish balls.

AFTERNOON

Return to Bamrung Muang Road and head west. Straight ahead stands the **Lak Muang** *(see p69)* shrine where you can watch supplicants making offerings and praying to Bangkok's city pillar. Wander west again between Sanam Luang and **Wat Phra Kaeo** *(see pp12–13)*, to admire paintings at the **Silpakorn University Art Exhibition Hall** *(see p73)*. Buy a lucky charm at the fascinating **Amulet Market** or in the small lanes off it. Have a cool drink at **S&P Restaurant** *(see p75)* by the riverside Tha Maharaj mall at Maharat Pier to round off your day's wander in the Old City.

See map on p68

The Best of the Rest

1 Wat Ratchabophit
MAP C4 ▪ Fuang
Nakhon Road ▪ 02 221
1888 ▪ Open 5am–8pm
daily; ordination hall:
open 9–9:30am &
5:30–6pm daily
The highlights here (see
p41) include inlay work on
the doors and windows
of the *bot* (ordination hall), and
colorful tiles in the cloisters.

**Inlay work at
Wat Ratchabophit**

**2 Bamrung
Muang Road**
MAP D4
Originally an elephant trail, this was
one of the first roads to be paved in
Bangkok. Its shops sell temple neces-
sities such as monks' robes, candles,
incense, and Buddha images.

3 Museum of Siam
MAP C5 ▪ Sanam Chai Road
▪ 02 225 2777 ▪ Open 10am–6pm
Tue–Sun ▪ Adm ▪ www.museum
siam.org
Spread over three floors, this museum
has fascinating interactive exhibits
that explore Thai history and culture,
Buddhism, and more.

4 Phra Sumen Fort
MAP C2 ▪ Phra Athit Road
This octagonal brick-and-stucco fort,
one of 14 watchtowers, was built in
1783 to defend the city from attack.

**Phra Sumen
Fort**

5 Wat Mahathat
MAP B3 ▪ Maharat
Road ▪ 02 221 5999
▪ Open 7am–8pm daily
This royal temple (see
p40) is home to the
respected Vipassana
Meditation Center.

**6 National
Gallery**
MAP C3 ▪ 4 Chao Fa Road
▪ 02 281 2224 ▪ Open
9am–4pm Wed–Sun ▪ Adm
Located in a building that
once housed the Royal Mint, this
is Bangkok's principal art gallery.
It features the work of established
and emerging Thai artists.

7 Khao San Road
MAP C3
Besides several budget guesthouses,
this bustling backpacker hub
has a variety of souvenir shops,
market stalls, and restaurants.

8 Wat Bowoniwet
MAP C2 ▪ 240 Phra Sumen
Road ▪ 02 280 0869 ▪ Open 8am–
5pm daily ▪ www.watbowon.org
The base of the Thammayut sect
of Buddhism, this temple (see p40)
has some striking murals.

**9 Loha Prasat and Wat
Ratchanadda**
MAP D3 ▪ 2 Maha Chai Road ▪ 02
224 8807 ▪ Open 9am–5pm daily
The Loha Prasat (or "iron castle")
is a stepped, seven-tiered pyramid
with 37 metal spires. Its grounds
are shared with Wat Ratchanadda.

**10 King Prajadhipok
(Rama VII) Museum**
MAP D3 ▪ 2 Lan Luang Road
▪ 02 280 3413 ▪ Open 9am–4pm
Tue–Sun
This museum looks at the reign
of Rama VII (1925–35), which saw
the transition of Siam from absolute
to constitutional monarchy.

Quiet Corners

1 Buddhaisawan Chapel, National Museum

After learning about Thai history in the National Museum *(see p16)*, settle down on the cool teak floorboards of this chapel to meditate, in front of the Phra Sihing Buddha image.

Artwork, Buddhaisawan Chapel

2 Sanam Luang

This open grassy area *(see p69)* has several benches in the shade of trees that offer rest to weary legs.

3 Massage Pavilion, Wat Pho

Traditional Thai massage is a great help for aching legs. Come here *(see p18)* for some of the country's best masseurs.

4 Thammasat University
MAP B3 ■ Maharat Road

Thailand's second-oldest university, opened in 1934, lies just upstream from the Amulet Market. There are some nice spots for resting, and a food court catering to the students.

5 Santichaiprakhan Park
MAP C2 ■ Phra Athit Road
■ Open 5am–10pm daily

Looking out over the Chao Phraya River, this park makes an excellent place to sit and see the world go by. Visitors can also join the aerobics class held here at dusk every day.

6 Romaninart Park
MAP D4 ■ Maha Chai Road
■ Open 5am–9pm daily

Formerly the site of a prison, this park now has ponds, fountains, and shaded paths.

7 Silpakorn University Art Exhibition Hall
MAP B4 ■ Na Phra Lan Road
■ 02 221 3841 ■ Open 9am–pm Mon–Fri, 9am–4pm Sat

Set inside the country's leading art school, this tranquil gallery features works by teachers, students, and artists-in-residence at the university.

8 Mahakan Fort
MAP D3 ■ Maha Chai and Ratchadamnoen roads

This octagonal fort is one of two surviving watchtowers of the 14 that ringed the city in the late 18th century. The park beside it is a great place to stop and relax.

9 Riverside Restaurants, Tha Maharaj
MAP B3 ■ Maharat Road

The cool river breeze makes this complex of restaurants in Tha Maharaj shopping mall, is one of the best places to recover from a tiring walk.

Walking in tranquil Saranrom Park

10 Saranrom Park
MAP C4 ■ Rachini Road
■ Open 5am–9pm daily

With shady trees, fountains, and benches, this park is a great place to take a break after trekking round the Grand Palace or Wat Pho *(see pp12–15)*.

See map on p68

Bars and Clubs

① Phra Nakorn
MAP C3 ■ 58/2 Soi Damnoen Klang Tai ■ 02 622 0282 ■ Open 6pm–1am daily

Popular with artists, this bar offers views of the Golden Mount from the roof terrace. The first floor features regular exhibitions.

Outdoor seating at Adhere the 13th

② Adhere the 13th (Blues Bar)
MAP C2 ■ 13 Samsen Road ■ 08 9769 4613 ■ Open 6pm–midnight daily

Small neighborhood bar (see p56) with live blues and jazz bands nightly.

③ Sheepshank
MAP B2 ■ Phra Athit express-boat pier ■ 02 629 5165 ■ Open 5pm–1am Mon, 11–1am Tue–Sun

A gastropub set in an old boat repair yard by the river, Sheepshank serves American and Japanese craft beers.

④ Hippie de Bar
MAP C3 ■ 46 Khao San Road ■ 08 1820 3762 ■ Open 4pm–2am daily

A fashionable courtyard bar and boutique with a retro look, Hippie de Bar attracts a diverse crowd.

⑤ Brick Bar
MAP C3 ■ 265 Khao San Road ■ Open 6:30–11pm daily ■ www.brickbarkhaosan.com

This is a popular live music club on Khao San Road, frequented by locals and travelers alike.

⑥ The Club
MAP C3 ■ 123 Khao San Road ■ 02 629 1010 ■ Open 10pm–3am daily

A lively atmosphere, vast dance floor, and music from techno to trance pull in the crowds here.

⑦ Bottle Rocket
MAP C2 ■ 76/1 Phra Arthit Road ■ 08 6085 5550 ■ Open 5pm–midnight Tue–Sun

A small bar, Bottle Rocket offers Thai, Japanese as well as international craft beers on tap, and in bottles.

⑧ Madame Musur
MAP C2 ■ Soi Ram Bhuttri ■ 02 281 4238 ■ Open 9am–midnight daily

The ambience is relaxed at Madame Musur. It serves northern Thai food and a variety of drinks.

⑨ Roof Bar
MAP C3 ■ 3rd floor, Centre Point Plaza, Khao San Road ■ 08 6777 1117 ■ Open 4:30pm–1:30am daily

Watch live bands with an amazing view from the balcony. It's a great spot to enjoy fresh air and good fun.

⑩ Brown Sugar: The Jazz Boutique
MAP D3 ■ 469 Wanchad Junction, Phra Sumen Road ■ 02 282 0396 ■ Open 5pm–1am Tue–Thu & Sun, 5pm–2am Fri–Sat ■ www.brownsugarbangkok.com

Enjoy live music at one of Bangkok's famous jazz bars (see p56).

Brown Sugar: The Jazz Boutique

Restaurants

1 Mui Lee Chicken & Rice

MAP B5 ■ 275 Thanon Wang Doem ■ 08 8006 0012 ■ Open 8am–1:30pm Sun–Fri ■ B

A legendary street food joint near Wat Arun serving only Hainanese chicken rice. Get here early to avoid the lunchtime rush.

2 Kaloang Home Kitchen

MAP D1 ■ 2 Soi Wat Tevarakunchorn ■ 02 281 9228 ■ Open 11am–10pm daily ■ BB

Hidden behind the National Library, this simple, alfresco riverside venue offers guests an excellent menu of inexpensive Thai cuisine.

3 Methavalai Sorn Daeng

MAP D3 ■ 78/2 Ratchadamnoen Khlang Road ■ 02 224 3088 ■ Open 10:30am–10pm daily ■ BB

Open since 1957, and now a rewarded Michelin star restaurant, this place is popular with the older generation of Thais. Expect starched white table-cloths and delectable Thai cuisine.

4 S&P, Maharat Pier

MAP B3 ■ Maharat Pier ■ Open 10am–10pm daily ■ B

Part of a countrywide chain of restaurants, S&P turns out tasty Thai food, ice creams, and cakes. A breezy riverside terrace is part of the appeal at this branch.

5 Aquatini

MAP B2 ■ Navalai River Resort, 45 Phra Athit Road ■ 02 280 9955 ■ Open 6:30am–midnight daily ■ www.navalai.com ■ BB

On a breezy riverfront deck, this hotel restaurant *(see p115)* serves reasonably priced Thai food, especially seafood.

6 Hemlock

MAP B2 ■ 56 Phra Athit Road ■ 02 282 7507 ■ Open 3pm–midnight Mon–Sat ■ BB

A small, trendy café, Hemlock offers many unusual dishes, including several vegetarian options.

7 Supanniga Eating Room

MAP B5 ■ Riva Arun Hotel, 392/25–26 Maharat Road ■ 02 714 7608 ■ Open 11am–10pm Mon–Fri, 7:30am–10pm Sat & Sun ■ BB

This riverside restaurant-bar serves dishes from northern Thailand as well as flavorful cuisine of Chanthaburi.

Dining area at Supanniga Eating Room

8 Tham Na

MAP C3 ■ 175 Samsen Road ■ 02 282 4979 ■ Open 11am–9pm Mon–Sat, 9am–3pm Sun ■ www.maykaidee.com ■ BB

Good-value vegetarian restaurant, with regional ingredients like pomelo and lotus root featured in soups, salads, and curries.

9 Somsong Pochana

MAP C2 ■ 173 Samsen Road ■ Open 9am–4pm daily ■ B

Traditional Sukhothai-style noodles are served at this excellent lunch spot.

10 Krua Apsorn

MAP D3 ■ Dinsor Road ■ 02 685 4531 ■ Open Mon–Sat 10:30am–8pm ■ B

A simple restaurant, Krua Apsorn is perfect to sample traditional and varied Thai cuisine, especially seafood.

See map on p68

🔟 Chinatown

At the time of Bangkok's founding in 1782, Chinese immigrants were forced out of Rattanakosin Island to make way for the Grand Palace and government buildings. They settled to the south of Rattanakosin Island beside the Chao Phraya River. These days Chinatown is one of the most lively areas of the city, and though it lacks the grand monuments of the Old City, it is fascinating for its maze of alleys, markets, colorful temples, and gold shops. Sharing this crowded part of the capital is a small Indian community in a sub-district known as Little India, with the cloth market of Phahurat at its heart.

Golden Buddha, Wat Traimit

1 Golden Buddha, Wat Traimit

MAP F6 ■ 661 Charoen Krung Road ■ 02 225 9775 ■ Open 8am–5pm daily ■ Adm

There are thousands of gold-leaf smothered Buddha images in Thailand, but the Golden Buddha is made of solid gold – all 12,000 lb (5,500 kg) of it. This fact was revealed only in 1955 when it was accidentally dropped, exposing its gold interior. The 13-ft (4-m) tall, 13th-century Sukhothai Buddha is housed in a glittering, three-story shrine.

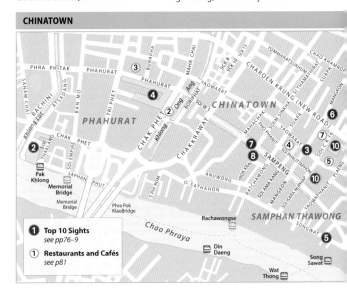

CHINATOWN

1 **Top 10 Sights**
see pp76–9

1 **Restaurants and Cafés**
see p81

2 Pak Khlong Market

MAP C5 ■ Chakphet Road ■ Open 24 hours daily

The sights, sounds, and smells at this bustling flower, fruit, and vegetable market threaten to cause sensory overload. Throughout the night, boats laden with jasmine, lotus, and carnations unload their cargo, and at dawn the colorful displays of blooms and tropical fruits are at their best. The market is at its busiest in the mornings.

Gold shops along Yaowarat Road

3 Yaowarat Road

MAP E5 ■ Shops: open 8am–10pm daily

The heart of Chinatown's gold trade, this one-way street has over 100 gold shops. Painted bright red, these shops flaunt glittering displays of necklaces and bracelets. The high volume of vehicles here often makes traffic come to a complete halt, and each evening the street gets even busier as foodstalls and vendors occupy every inch of space available.

4 Phahurat Market (Little India)

MAP C5 ■ Phahurat Road ■ Open 9am–6pm daily

Crossing the road in Bangkok's Chinatown can seem like traveling from China to India in the blink of an eye. An enclave within an enclave, Little India, mostly concentrated along Phahurat Road and the block to the south, is a thriving hub of commerce. Saris and rainbow-colored bolts of cloth are stacked to the rooftops of the cramped shophouses and spill onto the streets. Tiny teahouses and shops selling offerings for Hindu temples complete the scene.

5 Songwat Road

MAP E6

Songwat Road runs parallel to the Chao Phraya River (see pp20–21), and though the riverside piers and wharves are less busy now than a century ago, many companies still have their warehouses in this area, especially those in the rice trade. A stroll along this road and the small lanes that lead down to the river conjures up something of the atmosphere of Chinatown in bygone days. At its western end, Songwat Road leads to Pak Khlong, the flower market.

Wat Mangkon Kamalawat, Chinatown's most revered temple

6 Wat Mangkon Kamalawat (Wat Leng Noi Yee)

MAP E5 ■ Charoen Krung Road ■ 02 222 3975 ■ Open 6am–6pm daily

Established in 1871, this is the most important of Chinatown's many Chinese temples. Wat Mangkon Kamalawat, or Dragon Flower Temple, is particularly active during the Vegetarian Festival in October, when devotees flock here to make offerings. Also known as Wat Leng Noi Yee, it has an impressive entrance gateway and the complex contains Buddhist, Taoist, and Confucian shrines. It is constantly busy with people making offerings, and vendors selling religious goods outside the temple doing a brisk business.

YAOWARAT GOLD

The strong Chinese influence on Thai culture is evident in the prevalence of gold shops in the city, gold being a traditionally Chinese commodity. In Bangkok, gold is sold not by ounce but by baht, and some see it as more reliable than the country's currency. Many also wear gold bracelets and thick linked watch straps as a sign of their status.

7 Sampeng Lane

MAP L3 ■ Open 8am–8pm daily

This narrow, frenetic lane, also known as Soi Wanit 1, stretches for about half a mile (1 km) through the very heart of Chinatown and is not for the fainthearted. Cars cannot even squeeze their way down here, but motorbikes and porters carrying stacks of goods try to weave through the slow-moving sea of people. People pause every few steps to examine the goods on offer – from computer games, to toys and clothes.

8 Wat Ga Buang Kim

MAP D6 ■ Trok Krai, Anuwong Road

Set around a small, enclosed courtyard, this neighborhood temple is remarkable for its beautifully ornamented "vegetarian hall," which has an altar framed by intricately carved, gold-painted miniatures. The hall's outer wall is decorated with tableaux as well, and finely crafted ceramic figurines drawn from Chinese opera stories adorn the doorway at the top of the stairs. A second building in the temple compound functions as a stage for Chinese opera performances.

9 Hua Lampong Station
MAP F6 ■ Rama IV Road
■ 02 225 6964

Initiated by Rama V *(see p38)*, Hua Lampong Station was built just before World War I by Dutch architects. Despite several revamps since then, the basic shell remains unchanged, making this train station one of Bangkok's most easily recognizable landmarks. For a long time, the station was the place where many visitors began their Bangkok experience, but in 2022 railway operations ceased here and were moved to the new Bang Sue station. There are plans underway to turn the Hua Lampong building into a museum.

10 Talad Kao and Talad Mai
MAP E6 ■ Soi Isara Nuphap
■ Talad Kao: open 4–11am daily;
Talad Mai: open 4am–6pm daily

These two fresh-produce markets are piled high with fish, mushrooms, mangoes, curry pastes, Chinese herbs, and spices. The Talad Kao, or Old Market, has been open for trade since the late 18th century, while the Talad Mai, or New Market, is about 100 years old. Together, they have earned themselves a good name for high-quality meat, fish, vegetables, and fruits. They remain particularly busy during the Chinese New Year. The old market is frantic at dawn, but winds down before lunchtime, while the new one continues to operate until evening.

Hawkers at Talad Mai market

EXPLORING CHINATOWN AND LITTLE INDIA

▶ MORNING

Traffic can be a nightmare at any time in Chinatown, so take the public ferry to Tha Rachini, at around 9am. Take the first right on leaving the pier, cross the canal and go right again into **Pak Khlong Market** *(see p77)*, which should be at its busiest and best at this time. Next, head north up Atsadang Road and then turn right into Phra Phitak Road. Within a couple of short blocks this becomes **Phahurat Road**, *(see p77)* and you are transported to Little India. Keep walking straight through until you reach Chak Phet Road. Have a delicious north Indian lunch at the **Royal India** *(see p81)* restaurant.

AFTERNOON

With your batteries recharged, plunge into **Sampeng Lane** with its kitsch gadgets and wind-up toys. Make sure that your wallet or purse is well hidden as this is a pickpocket's paradise. When you reach Soi Isara Nuphap, turn left and wander past all the Chinese herbalists and pharmacists on your way to **Yaowarat Road** *(see p77)*. Turn right here and notice the profusion of gold shops, all painted bright red with vibrant gold lettering, and most with an armed guard on duty. Where Yaowarat Road meets Charoen Krung Road, cross to the east side of the street and enter the temple of **Wat Traimit** *(see p76)*. Sit down for a few moments to rest and admire the superb craftsmanship of the **Golden Buddha** *(see p76)* and enjoy a tranquil end to the day.

See map on pp76–7

What to Buy

1 Flowers
Pak Khlong Market (see p77) is the place to buy fresh flowers – either individual cut blooms or a bouquet mixing a few favorites. Temperate flowers such as roses mingle with orchids and lotus ginger.

2 Gold
If you are seeking some gold ornamentation, check out the gold shops along Yaowarat Road (see p77), which sell 23-carat gold in a wide variety of designs.

Freshly-cut lotus buds

3 Textiles
The fantastic range of textiles on sale in Chinatown, and particularly in Phahurat Market (see p77), is enough to tempt many visitors to take home a bolt of cloth or some inexpensive ready-made garments.

Shop staff preparing packets of tea

4 Tea
Green tea and black tea, loose or packaged, is sold through-out Chinatown, and is consumed in great quantities by the Chinese themselves. Fresh markets and herbalists would be the best places for you to sniff out a good brew.

5 Incense
For the Chinese, incense is essential, particularly for making offerings, and several shops in Chinatown sell incense in coils, pyramids, small sticks, and big sticks that burn for hours.

6 Fashion Accessories
There is nothing exclusive about the cheap trinkets on sale throughout Chinatown, particularly along Sampeng Lane (see p78). Plastic ear-rings, strings of beads, cuddly mobile phone covers, and sequined handbags are just a few of the items on offer.

7 Ceramics
Most of the ceramics on sale in Chinatown are functional rather than decorative, yet the ceramic shops are worth nosing around for unexpected treasures.

8 Lanterns
In a few of the narrow alleys off Soi Isara Nuphap some families still make traditional Chinese lanterns for a living. Shops along Sampeng Lane sell the finished product in a range of bright colors.

9 Spices
Visitors to any of the fresh markets in Chinatown can admire colorful chili pastes and spices overflowing from huge enamel basins and pick out a few to experiment with at home.

10 Temple Offerings
The most common temple offerings in Bangkok are incense and colored paper, although shops specializing in religious necessities in Chinatown also sell miniature shrines and bright robes to drape around Chinese deities.

See map on pp76–7

Restaurants and Cafés

1 Haze BKK
MAP M2 ▪ 425 Luang Road
▪ 09 656 5635 ▪ Open 5–11pm Wed–Mon ▪ BB

Craft beer, both Thai and international, is accompanied by live music and big-screen sports at this laid-back bar.

2 Royal India
MAP D5 ▪ 392/1 Chak Phet Road ▪ 02 221 6565 ▪ Open 10am–10pm daily ▪ BB

Set in a back alley, Royal India scores low on decor, but serves diners some great north Indian dishes.

3 Food Center, Old Siam Plaza
MAP C5 ▪ Phahurat Road ▪ Open 10am–5pm daily ▪ B

On the third floor of Old Siam Plaza, the food court serves a good range of Thai and Chinese dishes, while the first floor stalls sell Thai desserts.

4 Shangarila
MAP E5 ▪ 306 Yaowarat Road ▪ 02 224 5933 ▪ Open 10:30am–10pm daily ▪ BB

One of a chain of popular Cantonese restaurants, this huge place serves great fare, including *dim sum*, soups, and stir-fries.

Delicious fare at Shangarila

PRICE CATEGORIES

For a meal for one with one or two dishes and a soft drink, including service.

B under B200   **BB** B200–1,000
BBB over B1,000

---

5 Hua Seng Hong
MAP E5 ▪ 371 Yaowarat Road ▪ 02 222 7053 ▪ Open 9–1am daily ▪ BB

Famed for its tasty bird's nest soup, Hua Seng Hong also offers dishes such as *hoy tawt* (mussels in batter).

6 T & K
MAP E6 ▪ 49 Soi Phadungdao ▪ 02 223 4519 ▪ Open 4:30pm–2am daily ▪ BB

A busy Chinatown restaurant, T & K specializes in barbecued seafood.

7 Hong Kong Noodles
MAP E5 ▪ 136/4 Soi Charoen Krung 16 ▪ Open 10am–8pm daily ▪ B

This is a bustling, popular restaurant specializing in roast duck noodles.

8 Chong Kee
MAP F6 ▪ 84 Soi Sukon 1, Trimit Road ▪ Open 9:30am–2pm Mon, 9:30am–5:30pm Tue–Sun ▪ B

Customers flock here for the house specialty – pork satay on sweet toast.

9 Tep Bar
MAP M3 ▪ Soi Nana (near Charoen Krung Road) ▪ (09) 8467 2944 ▪ Open 5pm–midnight Sun–Thu, 5pm–1am Fri & Sat ▪ BB

On artsy Soi Nana, Tep offers delicious food including grilled meats and spicy salads. Also try their Thai herbal whiskey.

10 Ba Hao
MAP M3 ▪ 8 Soi Nana (near Charoen Krung Road) ▪ 06 4635 1989 ▪ Open 6pm–midnight Tue–Sun ▪ BB

Tuck into Chinese comfort food, teas, ginseng shots, and cocktails at this chic Chinoiserie.

TOP10 Downtown

Bangkok's Downtown area radiates out eastward from the Old City and Chinatown. This densely built-up area includes embassies and offices as well as top hotels, restaurants, and entertainment venues. There are a few historical sights, including the Assumption Cathedral, and some gorgeous traditional houses that contrast with all the surrounding skyscrapers. Lush Lumphini Park provides an escape from the concrete jungle, while Silom Road, Siam Square, and Ploenchit are the best shopping areas. Silom is also one of the city's liveliest areas for nightlife; along its infamous side streets, Patpong 1 and 2, market stalls, and bars feature live bands.

**Prehistoric pottery,
Suan Pakkad**

Previous pages A demon guard at the Grand Palace and Wat Phra Kaeo complex

1 Patpong

MAP P5 ▪ Between Silom and
Surawong roads ▪ Markets and bars
open 6pm–1am daily

Named after a Chinese millionaire
who first started to develop these
narrow lanes, Patpong 1 and 2
became world famous when their
go-go bars were visited by US soldiers
on leave from Vietnam in the late
1960s. Its heyday was in the 1980s,
during Thailand's first tourist boom.
In the early 1990s, a night market
was set up along the length of
Patpong 1, and the adult entertainment venues began to decline.
A number of adult entertainment
venues still remain, however, and
touts are very common in the area.

The elaborate Assumption Cathedral

2 Assumption Cathedral

MAP M6 ▪ Soi Oriental ▪ Open
6am–7pm daily ▪ www.assumption
cathedralbkk.org

In quiet backstreets near the river, this
imposing building, erected in 1910,
replaced a structure from the 1820s. It
dominates a tree-lined square that is
part of a Catholic mission. The elaborate pink and white exterior matches
the bright Rococo interior. The cathedral bears testimony to the success
of French missions to Bangkok in the
19th century. While they made few
conversions, they managed to secure
religious tolerance for all.

3 The Queen Saovabha Memorial Institute

MAP P4 ▪ 1871 Rama IV Road
▪ Shows: 11am & 2pm Mon–Fri,
11am Sat & Sun ▪ Adm ▪ www.
saovabha.org

One of Bangkok's quirkier sights,
Queen Saovabha Memorial Institute
(see p50) was set up in 1923 as
the Pasteur Institute. The Thai
Red Cross runs it now, producing
serums for snake bites and promoting education about snakes.
During live demonstrations,
snakes are milked of their venom.

4 Erawan Shrine
MAP Q3 ▪ **Corner of Ratchadamri and Ploenchit roads**

An island of spirituality in a sea of commerce, the Erawan Shrine is one of Bangkok's quirkiest sights, with the Skytrain zipping by and shopping malls hemming it in. Thailand's most famous spirit house gained its fame in 1956 when its installation was credited with halting a string of fatal accidents at the construction site of the former Erawan Hotel. A constant stream of suppli-cants offer marigolds, incense, and candles, along with silent wishes.

Erawan Shrine

5 Suan Pakkad
MAP Q1 ▪ **352–354 Si Ayutthaya Road** ▪ **02 246 1775–6** ▪ **Open 9am–4pm daily** ▪ **Adm** ▪ **www.suanpakkad.com/main_eng.php**

This compound of traditional houses was assembled in the 1950s by Prince and Princess Chumbhot on former farmland (the name means "cabbage patch"). The museum has a varied collection of statues, paintings, porcelain, *khon* theater masks, and musical instruments.

6 Lumphini Park
MAP Q4 ▪ **Corner of Ratchadamri and Rama IV roads** ▪ **Open 5am–8pm daily**

It is difficult to imagine how Bangkok might be without this green lung that occupies a huge block in the heart of the commercial and entertain-ment district. Consisting of a large lake, well-tended lawns, and shady trees, it is busy from dawn with locals walking, jogging, and performing t'ai chi in groups. From February to April, it is a popular site for kite-flying.

7 Oriental Hotel
MAP M5 ▪ **48 Oriental Avenue** ▪ **02 659 9000** ▪ **www.mandarinoriental.com/bangkok**

Bangkok's oldest hotel enjoys double billing as both historic sight and luxurious accommodation option. It has hosted several famous writers, including Joseph Conrad and Somerset Maugham, in the Authors' Wing. Built in 1876, this original part of the hotel is now dwarfed by the Garden and River Wings, but still attracts visitors for afternoon tea in its Authors' Lounge.

8 Siam Square
MAP P2 ▪ **Corner of Rama I and Phaya Thai roads**

Flanked by multistory malls, Siam Square is a grid of streets packed with shopping arcades. The numer-ous tiny shops, some with no more than a meter frontage, make it a popular shopping area, especially for students from the neighboring Chulalongkorn University, who congregate around Center Point's milk bars and fast-food outlets at the southern end of the square. There are also shops selling designer clo-thes and fashion accessories, the creation of enterprising young Thai designers, plus a good selection of cafés, restaurants, and cinemas.

The lake at Lumphini Park

M. R. Kukrit's serene home

9 M. R. Kukrit's Heritage Home

MAP P6 ▪ Soi 7, Narathiwat Ratchanakarin Road ▪ 02 286 8185 ▪ Open 10am–4pm daily ▪ Adm

Descended from Rama II *(see p31)*, Mom Rajawongse Kukrit Pramoj (1911–95) was one of the best-loved Thais of the 20th century. He founded the newspaper *Siam Rath* and wrote hundreds of plays, poems, and novels. He even served as Prime Minister in 1975–6. His house, with many beautiful artworks and a garden, is preserved as he left it.

THAI SILK

Thailand's silk industry is world-famous, with a history going back some 3,000 years. It was, however, in decline when American businessman Jim Thompson arrived in Bangkok in the 1940s. He was determined to revive the industry and his business model, which allowed employees to work from home, empowered many Thai women, who could become breadwinners while also maintaining their homes.

10 Jim Thompson House

One of the most popular sights in Bangkok, this beautiful compound of traditional Thai houses *(see pp28–9)* allows visitors to imagine how life in a well-to-do, mid-20th century Bangkok home might have been. The evocative furnishings, sculptures, and tapestries give the building a refined character. Visitors to the house must join a guided tour, which are regular and in several languages.

A WALK THROUGH THE OLD FARANG QUARTER

 MORNING

Begin this half-mile (1-km) walking tour at the upscale **River City Shopping Complex**, on the riverfront just north of the pier at Tha Si Phraya. You will find jewelry, books, restaurants, clothes, and more. On the third and fourth floor are shops selling rare antiques, and an antiques auction is held every second month. From here head back south, passing the **Royal Orchid Sheraton** *(see p114)* to glimpse the **Portuguese Embassy**. Operational from 1820, this was the first embassy to be established in Siam by any European power. Follow the lane out to Charoen Krung Road and turn right to reach the **General Post Office**, a massive Art Deco building. Walk south along Charoen Krung from the post office and turn right into Soi 34 to see old wooden houses; the winding lane leads to **Haroon Mosque**, a small, attractive stucco building used by the local Muslim population. The next lane south, Soi 36, is home to the **French Embassy**, which was the second embassy to be established in Bangkok. Walk south, crossing Soi 38 and 40 to reach the **Assumption Cathedral** *(see p85)*. From the cathedral, follow an alley west towards the river, where the former headquarters of the East Asiatic Company, built in 1901, still stands. Have tea and cakes in the Authors' Lounge at the historic **Oriental Hotel** next door to end your morning's walk.

See map on pp84–5

The Best of the Rest

1 Pratunam Market
MAP Q1 ■ Corner of Phetburi and Ratchaprarop roads ■ Open 9am–midnight daily

Famous for its inexpensive textiles and ready-made clothes, Pratunam Market is a great place to witness the city's chaotic street life.

2 Maha Uma Devi Temple
MAP N5 ■ Corner of Silom Road and Soi Pan ■ 02 238 4007 ■ Open 6am–8pm daily

Also known as Sri Mariamman, this temple features a panoply of brightly painted Hindu deities above the entrance and around the interior walls.

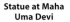

Statue at Maha Uma Devi

3 Baiyoke Sky Hotel
MAP Q1 ■ 222 Ratchaprarop Road ■ 02 656 3000 ■ Open 10–2am daily ■ Adm

Bangkok's second-tallest building at 1,000 ft (304 m), this tower has an open-air, revolving roof deck that offers superb panoramas of the city.

4 Royal Bangkok Sports Club
MAP Q3 ■ Henri Dunant Road ■ 02 028 7272 ■ www.rbsc.org

This attractive horse-racing club has a golf course set inside the track.

5 Neilson Hays Library
MAP N5 ■ 195 Suriwong Road ■ 02 233 1731 ■ Open 9:30am–5pm Tue–Sun ■ www.neilsonhayslibrary.org

Located in a historical building, this haven for bookworms has over 20,000 volumes on its shelves.

6 Chao Mae Tubtim Shrine
MAP R2 ■ Wireless Road

This eye-catching shrine (see p52) is encircled by phallic offerings from devotees wishing for fertility or prosperity.

7 Chulalongkorn University
MAP P3 ■ Phaya Thai Road ■ 02 215 0871 ■ www.chula.ac.th

The campus of Thailand's oldest and most respected university mixes Western and Thai architectural styles.

8 SEA LIFE Bangkok Ocean World
MAP P2 ■ Basement, Siam Paragon, Rama I Road ■ 02 687 2000 ■ Open 10am–9pm daily ■ Adm ■ www.sealifebangkok.com

This aquarium, home to over 400 species of marine life, features an underwater tunnel.

9 Museum of Counterfeit Goods
MAP T6 ■ Tilleke & Gibbins, Supalai Grand Tower, Rama III Road ■ 02 056 5548 ■ Open by appointment

Quirky displays of over 4,000 fake items, including clothing and drugs.

10 King Power Mahanakhon
MAP P5 ■ Narathiwat Ratchanakharin Road ■ Open 10am–midnight daily ■ Adm

Currently Thailand's second tallest building, this place has an observation deck at 1,030 ft (314 m).

King Power Mahanakhon

Shopping Malls

1 Siam Paragon
MAP P2 ▪ Rama I Road, Siam Square ▪ 02 610 8000 ▪ Open 10am–10pm daily ▪ www.siamparagon.co.th
With six floors of designer boutiques, bookshops, cinemas, restaurants, and fitness centers, this mall is one of the most popular in Bangkok.

2 Siam Center and Siam Discovery Center
MAP P2 ▪ Rama I Road ▪ 02 658 1000 ▪ Open 10am–10pm daily
Known for designer brands, trendy shops, and restaurants, these two adjoining malls attract young adults. Look out for local fashion labels such as Greyhound, Baking Soda, and Theatre.

3 Narai Phand
MAP Q2 ▪ President Tower, 973 Ploenchit Road ▪ 02 656 0398 ▪ Open 10am–8pm daily
At this government-sponsored shop for promoting quality Thai handi-crafts, everything is sold at fixed prices: woodcarvings, lacquerware, silk clothing, silverware, and more.

4 Peninsula Plaza
MAP Q3 ▪ 153 Ratchadamri Road ▪ 02 254 3320 ▪ Open 10am–8pm daily
This mall consists mostly of jewelers and designer outlets.

5 Central World
MAP Q2 ▪ 4/1–2 Ratchadamri Road ▪ 02 640 7000 ▪ Open 10am–10pm daily ▪ www.centralworld.co.th
Huge shopping complex (see p60) with fashion boutiques, home decor outlets, a bowling alley, and cinemas.

6 Erawan Bangkok
MAP Q3 ▪ 494 Ploenchit Road ▪ 02 250 7777 ▪ Open 10am–9pm daily ▪ www.erawanbangkok.com
Next to the Erawan Shrine, this luxury mall has plenty of boutiques by famous names, as well as classy cafés and a wellness center.

The stylish Gaysorn Village

7 Gaysorn Village
MAP Q2 ▪ Ploenchit Road ▪ 02 656 1149 ▪ Open 10am–10pm daily
International luxury brands and a few local designer stores display their wares here.

8 Mahboonkrong (MBK)
MAP P3 ▪ Phaya Thai Road ▪ Open 10am–10pm daily ▪ www.mbk-center.co.th
Packed with seven floors of fashions, accessories, electronics, cosmetics, jewelry, and restaurants, MBK (see p60) feels like a cross between a street market and a shopping mall.

9 EmQuartier
MAP T6 ▪ 693 Sukhumvit Road ▪ 02 269 1188 ▪ Open 10am–10pm daily ▪ www.emporium.co.th
Across the street from the Emporium (see p61), this mall has a less formal atmosphere and many boutiques.

10 Emporium
MAP T6 ▪ 622 Sukhumvit Road ▪ 02 269 1000 ▪ Open 10am–10pm daily ▪ www.emporium.co.th
An upscale mall, Emporium (see p61) features a department store, designer boutiques, restaurants, and cafés.

See map on pp84–5

Ways to Enjoy the River

1 Chao Phraya Express Boats

www.chaophrayaexpressboat.com
This extensive public transport system is both picturesque and useful. There are several color-coded routes, and the website explains everything.

2 Loy Nava Cruise

MAP M5 ▪ Si Phraya Pier ▪ 02 437 4932 ▪ Cruise 6–8pm & 8:10–10:10pm ▪ BBB
Choose from traditional, seafood, and vegetarian Thai dishes, then sit back and enjoy the fare on this rice barge as it chugs up and down the Chao Phraya River.

3 Anantara Sleep-on-Board Cruise to Ayutthaya

bangkok-cruises.anantara.com
The Anantara hotel group offers luxurious three-day cruises up the Chao Phraya to Ayutthaya, with accommodation aboard their lavishly refurbished teak rice barges. Although this is an expensive trip, it is a memorable experience.

Anantara sleep-on-board cruise

4 Canal Tours

These can be arranged with a tour agency or by negotiating with the boat captains directly. Good stops are the Royal Barge Museum (see p96) and the artist's house at Khlong Bang Luang (see p62).

5 Hotel and Other Free Shuttles

Just west of the BTS Saphan Taksin station, take a shuttle voyage to one of the spectacular riverside hotels on the Thonburi bank – such as the Millennium Hilton or the Anantara – for a meal or drink.

6 Charter Long-Tail Boat to Koh Kret

At any riverside pier, enterprising long-tail boat captains offer their vessels for hire. If you have a group of four or more, a visit to Koh Kret (see p95) would make for an excellent day trip. Agree a price, and pay upon returning to your point of origin.

7 Manohra Cruise

MAP S6 ▪ Anantara Bangkok Riverside Pier ▪ 02 476 0022 ▪ Cruise 7:30–9:30pm ▪ www.manohra cruises.com ▪ BBB
Operating out of the Anantara Bangkok Riverside, this cruise offers guests tasty curries and stir-fries.

8 Grand Pearl Cruise

MAP M5 ▪ River City Pier ▪ 02 861 0255 ▪ Cruise 7:30–9:30pm ▪ www.grandpearlcruise.com ▪ BBB
This cruise is perfect for those looking for a lively evening. Boats are big and offer live music and lounge areas, plus a blowout buffet.

9 Taking the Boat to Bang Krajao

This oasis of clean air and greenery (see p97) can be reached by a public boat from behind Wat Khlong Toey Nok or by chartering a private long-tail from anywhere on the river.

10 Yok Yor Cruise

MAP L4 ▪ Soi 20, Tha Din Daeng Road, Thonburi ▪ 02 863 0565 ▪ Cruise 8–10pm ▪ www.yokyor.co.th/english ▪ BB
Bangkok's only budget dinner cruise is popular but the menu is limited.

Restaurants

PRICE CATEGORIES

For a meal for one with one or two dishes and a soft drink, including service.

B under B200   **BB** B200–1,000
BBB over B1,000

① Le Normandie

MAP M5 ■ Mandarin Oriental Hotel, 48 Oriental Avenue ■ 02 659 9000 ■ Open noon–2pm & 7–10pm Mon–Sat ■ www.mandarinoriental.com/bangkok ■ BBB

The Brittany lobster and pan-fried duck liver are specialties of this French restaurant *(see p59)*.

② Ban Khun Mae

MAP P2 ■ 458/7–9 Siam Square Soi 8 ■ 02 250 1952 ■ Open 11am–11pm daily ■ BB

With its extensive menu of classic Thai dishes, Ban Khun Mae is an ideal spot for lunch or dinner.

③ Rang Mahal

MAP T6 ■ Rembrandt Hotel, 26th floor, Sukhumvit Soi 18 ■ 02 261 7050 ■ Open 5pm–midnight daily & 11am–2:30pm Sun ■ BB

Consistently named Bangkok's best Indian restaurant, Rang Mahal *(see p59)* serves elegant, traditional Northern Indian cuisine and has great views.

④ Liu

MAP R3 ■ Conrad Hotel, 87 Wireless Road ■ 02 690 9999 ■ Open 11:30am–2:30pm & 6–10:30pm daily ■ BB

This gourmet Chinese restaurant *(see p59)* serves classic regional cuisines – Cantonese, Shanghainese, Sichuan – with a contemporary twist.

⑤ Lenzi Tuscan Kitchen

MAP Q3 ■ Ruam Rudee Soi 2 ■ 02 001 0116 ■ Open 11:45am–2pm & 6–10:45pm daily ■ BB

Famous for several Italian restaurants, the chef focuses on native Tuscany dishes here *(see p59)*. Produce comes from the family farm near Pisa.

⑥ Breeze

MAP M6 ■ 52nd floor, State Tower, 1055 Silom Road ■ 02 624 9555 ■ Open 6–11pm daily ■ BBB

Come here for spectacular views and impeccable (but pricey) Asian food.

Incredible food and views at Breeze

⑦ Eat Me

MAP P5 ■ Soi Pipat 2, Convent Road ■ 02 238 0931 ■ Open 3pm–1am daily ■ BB

A very imaginative international fusion menu is offered here *(see p59)*.

⑧ Gaggan

MAP Q3 ■ 68/1 Soi Langsuan (opp Soi 3) ■ 02 652 1700 ■ Sittings at 5:30 & 9:30pm Mon–Sat ■ BBB

Gaggan *(see p59)* serves progressive Indian food.

⑨ Goji Kitchen and Bar

MAP T6 ■ 199 Soi Sukhumvit 22 ■ 020 595 999 ■ Open 11am–10pm daily ■ BBB

Goji is a celebrated pan-Asian restaurant in the Marriott Marquis Queen's Park hotel. Seating here is arranged around an open kitchen.

⑩ Issaya Siamese Club

MAP off R6 ■ 4 Soi Sri Aksorn, Chua Ploeng Road ■ 02 672 9040–1 ■ Open 11:30am–3pm & 6–10:30pm daily ■ BB

Housed in a mansion, this restaurant *(see p59)* serves Thai cuisine.

See map on pp84–5

Bars and Pubs

① Diplomat Bar
MAP R3 ■ Conrad Hotel, All Seasons Place, 87 Wireless Road (Witthayu) ■ 02 690 9244 ■ Open 7am–1am Sun–Thu, 7am–2am Fri & Sat

Unwind along with the high-flyers at this super-elegant bar while sipping a cocktail and enjoying the resident jazz band.

② The Zuk Bar
MAP Q5 ■ Sukhothai Hotel, 13/3 South Sathorn Road ■ 02 344 8888 ■ Open 5pm–1am Mon–Sat, 5pm–midnight Sun ■ www.sukhothai.com

Surrounded by gardens and lotus ponds, the bar at this elegant, low-rise hotel is a relaxing place for drinks at the end of a hot day, accompanied by Spanish hams, cheese platters and other tapas.

③ Moon Bar
MAP Q6 ■ Banyan Tree Hotel, South Sathorn Road ■ 02 679 1200 ■ Open 5pm–1am daily

Enjoy the fabulous views from high up above the city at Moon Bar, which offers a complete range of cocktails.

Spectacular views from Moon Bar

④ Bar@494
MAP Q3 ■ 494 Ratchadamri Road ■ 02 254 6250 ■ Open 3pm–midnight daily

The excellent wines and tapas are reasonably priced at this small bar in the Grand Hyatt Erawan.

⑤ Oskar Bistro
MAP T6 ■ 24 Sukhumvit Soi 11 ■ Open 4pm–2am daily ■ www.oskar-bistro.com

Great for a pre- or post-clubbing drink and snack, this stylish place has good craft beers and cocktails.

⑥ Sky Bar
MAP M6 ■ 63rd floor, State Tower, 1055 Silom Road ■ 02 624 9555 ■ Open 6pm–1am daily

Indulge in a pricey sundowner at the Sky Bar and admire the view.

⑦ Namsaah Bottling Trust
MAP P5 ■ Soi 7, Silom Road ■ 02 636 6622 ■ Open 5pm–1am daily

This retro-kitsch gastrobar in a bright pink, 100-year-old villa serves creative cocktails and great fusion food.

⑧ Small's
MAP Q6 ■ 186/3 Suan Phlu Soi 1 ■ 09 5585 1398 ■ Open 5–11pm Wed–Mon

Come here for the city's best whiskey selection. Light meals are served while jazz plays in the background.

⑨ Viva & Aviv The River
MAP M5 ■ Ground floor, River City shopping centre ■ Open noon–9pm Tue–Sun ■ www.vivaaviv.com

Wonderful cocktails, comfort food and a lovely river terrace are highlights of this riverside bar.

⑩ Hyde and Seek
MAP R3 ■ Athenée Residence, 65/1 Soi Ruam Rudee ■ Open 11am–1am daily ■ www.hydeandseek.com

This classy but lively gastrobar, has an appealing garden seating, and features DJs every night.

Nightclubs and Music Venues

The popular Hard Rock Café

1 Hard Rock Café
MAP P3 ▪ 424/3–6 Soi 11, Siam Square ▪ 02 658 4090 ▪ Open 11am–midnight daily

Popular worldwide, this is one of the city's liveliest night spots.

2 Bamboo Bar
MAP M5 ▪ Oriental Hotel, 48 Oriental Avenue ▪ 02 659 9000 ▪ Open 5pm–1:30am Fri & Sat (until 12:30am Sun–Thu) ▪ www.mandarinoriental.com/bangkok

With an excellent resident band this is a brilliant spot *(see p56)* for jazz lovers.

3 WOOBAR®
MAP P6 ▪ W Bangkok Hotel, 106 North Sathorn Road ▪ 02 344 4131 ▪ Open 9am–midnight daily

A variety of sounds, from techno to funky house, are played at this beautifully sophisticated hotel bar.

4 Mixx Discotheque
MAP Q2 ▪ President Tower Arcade, 973 Phloen Chit Road ▪ 02 656 0383 ▪ Open 10pm–2am daily ▪ Adm

Known for its superb acoustics and sound system, this club plays hip-hop, R&B, and house music.

5 Levels
MAP T6 ▪ Aloft Hotel, 6th floor, Sukhumvit Soi 11 ▪ (08) 2308 3246 ▪ Open 9pm–3am daily

Different styles of music play in each of this hot club's three party zones, which include a chill-out lounge bar.

6 The Club @ Koi
MAP N6 ▪ Sathorn Square Complex, 98 North Sathorn Road ▪ 02 108 2005 ▪ Open 6pm–2am Tue–Sat ▪ Adm on weekends

Downtown's most elegant dancing spot occupies the two top floors of a skyscraper. The music varies nightly.

7 DJ Station
MAP P5 ▪ Silom Soi 2 ▪ 02 266 4029 ▪ Open 9:30pm–2am daily ▪ Adm

Silom Soi 2 is dominated by gay clubs, and this three-floor nightclub is the most popular.

8 Maggie Choo's
MAP M5 ▪ Novotel Bangkok Fenix Silom Hotel, 320 Silom Road ▪ 091 772 2144 ▪ Open 6pm–3am daily

One of Bangkok's most imaginative nightspots, this has 1930s decor, live jazz, and good food on offer.

Jazz band at Maggie Choo's

9 Saxophone
MAP T6 ▪ 3/8 Phaya Thai Road ▪ 02 246 5472 ▪ Open 6pm–2am daily

A Bangkok music institution for 30 years, Saxophone offers live jazz, blues, and reggae. It's a friendly spot that serves excellent Thai food.

10 Sky Train Jazz Bar
MAP T6 ▪ Rangnam Alley, Thanon Phaya Thai ▪ 089 895 4299 ▪ Open 3–11pm daily

Buzzy rooftop bar overlooking Victory Monument and serving reasonably priced cocktails.

See map on pp84–5

TOP 10 Greater Bangkok

Most of Bangkok's suburban areas are housing estates, but there are also some unmissable sights, like Chatuchak Weekend Market. The former capital Thonburi has the enigmatic Wat Arun and the Royal Barge Museum. To the north of the Old City, Dusit features Wat Benjamabophit. East of the center lie Kamthieng House and the Rama IX Royal Park, while a short boat ride north, Nonthaburi and Koh Kret offer a taste of provincial Thailand.

Riverside Wat Arun

GREATER BANGKOK

1 Chatuchak Weekend Market

This market (see pp26–7) covers a massive area, with about 15,000 stalls selling a mind-boggling range of products, from plants to antiques and paintings. Considered to be the world's largest open-air market, Chatuchak is too big to see everything in a day, so pick up a map at the entrance and target the areas that interest you.

2 Wat Arun

This ancient temple (see pp30–31) in Thonburi, on the west bank of the Chao Phraya River (see pp20–21), is one of Bangkok's best-known icons with its five prangs (towers). These prangs are covered with broken shards of colorful porcelain that create an intriguing abstract pattern when viewed up close. The temple's bot (ordination hall) is also worth exploring, both for its murals and the exquisite Buddha image, which was apparently molded by King Rama II.

3 Koh Kret

MAP S4 ▪ 4 miles (7 km) N of Nonthaburi

Combining a trip to Nonthaburi (see p96) with an exploration of Koh Kret, an ox-bow island in a meander of the Chao Phraya River (see pp20–21), makes for an enjoyable day. Hire a longtail boat from Nonthaburi to reach Koh Kret. The island is inhabited by the Mon people, who make terra-cotta pots for sale in markets in the city. There are no cars, so you can listen to the twitter of birds as you wander around the island, passing mango, papaya, and durian plantations, pausing to watch busy potters at work, and perhaps picking up a sample of their work.

- **1** Top 10 Sights see pp94–7
- **1** Restaurants see p99
- **1** The Best of the Rest see p98
- **1** Bars and Pubs see p100
- **1** Nightclubs and Entertainment see p101

Temple on the island of Koh Kret

4 Soi Thonglor

MAP T6

Also known as Sukhumvit Soi 55, this area of east Bangkok is popular with young Thai professionals and expats. There's nothing of great cultural significance here, but the area has a fun vibe, with many restaurants, bars, and boutiques. Take BTS to Thonglor station, stroll a mile (1.6 km) up one side of the street and return on the other, taking in the lively cafés and entertainment venues.

Fruit and vegetable vendors spread out their produce in Nonthaburi market

5 Nonthaburi
MAP S4 ■ Nonthaburi Province

Take the express boat heading upstream from any pier in the city center and get off at the last stop in Nonthaburi. Here, the Wat Chalerm Phra Kiet temple, originally built by Rama III *(see p31)*, features intricate porcelain tilework on the doors and window frames of the *bot* (ordination hall). This region is famed for the superior quality of its durian fruit.

Phayathai Palace's cone-topped turret

6 Phayathai Palace
MAP H1 ■ Ratchawithi Road ■ 02 354 7987 ■ Tours 9:30am & 1:30pm Sat & Sun

This palace was built in 1909 as a royal country retreat. After the 1932 coup *(see p38)*, it was commandeered by the Thai military as a hospital (Phramongkutklao Hospital), which still functions around the palace today. The highlight of the palace is the Thewaratsaparom Throne Hall, which has beautifully carved pillars, balconies, and archways.

7 Kamthieng House
MAP T6 ■ 131 Sukhumvit Soi 21 ■ 02 661 6470–3 ■ Open 9am–5pm Tue–Sat ■ www.thesiamsociety.org

This beautiful Lanna house began life in the mid-19th century as the home of the Nimman-heimin family in Chiang Mai, but was carefully dismantled and reconstructed on this site in 1962 when it was donated to the Siam Society. Today it functions as an ethnological museum, with farming implements, a multimedia display on the Thai belief in spirits, a rural kitchen, and a granary with an exhibition on rice-farming rituals.

8 Royal Barge Museum
MAP A2 ■ Khlong Bangkok Noi ■ 02 424 0004 ■ Open 9am–5pm daily ■ Adm

This display of vessels offers a glimpse into the pageantry of the Thai monarchy. On rare ceremonial occasions, the elaborately decorated barges are propelled by bedecked oarsmen. The main barge on display, *Suphannahongse*, carries the Thai King and Queen at such times. It is carved out of a single teak tree. Its prow is adorned with a majestic golden swan.

⑨ Bang Krajao
MAP T6 ■ MRT to Khlong Toey, then taxi to pier behind Wat Khlong Toey Nok

Cycling is a great way to see this area, an oasis of traditional villages, mangrove forests, and fruit orchards on the west side of the Chao Phraya River. Bicycles can be hired at the pier. Nearby, the Sri Nakhon Kuenkhan Park has huge trees, landscaped gardens, and pavilions on a lake.

THE DREADED DURIAN

The durian, a most unusual fruit, arouses adoration and disgust in equal measure for its strong repelling smell and heavenly creamy taste. The spiky shell belies the soft yellow pods beneath it, cushioned by thick padding. The mushy texture and smooth, tangy taste take some getting used to, but once hooked there is no going back.

⑩ Rama IX Royal Park
MAP U6 ■ Sukhumvit Soi 103 ■ Open 5am–7pm daily ■ Adm

This is an ideal spot to head for when you need a break from Bangkok's relentless congestion. Though it takes a while to get to the park, on entering the sprawling site, the effort becomes worthwhile. The park was opened in 1987 to commemorate the 60th birthday of Rama IX *(see p39)*, and contains a museum explaining the life and achievements of the king, a large lake with pedal boats, as well as beautifully landscaped grounds with several unusual plants that are clearly labeled.

Rama IX Royal Park

EXPLORING CHATUCHAK AND THONBURI

▶ MORNING

Start before 8am and make your way to Mo Chit Skytrain station for a good look round **Chatuchak Weekend Market** *(see pp26–7)*. Pick up a map at the main entrance on the Phaholyothin Road and go straight ahead through the maze of stalls to the slender clocktower to orient yourself. Check out section 8 (handicrafts), browse handmade ceramics in sections 11–13, before stocking up your wardrobe in sections 10–21 (clothing and footwear). As there are thousands of foodstalls, you can refuel whenever you get hungry or thirsty.

AFTERNOON

At midday, return to Mo Chit Skytrain Station and take the Skytrain to Saphan Taksin. From here, take an express boat upriver to Tha Tien, then hop on one of the regular cross-river ferries to **Wat Arun** *(see pp30–31)*. Take a good look at the bright ceramics on the *prangs* (towers), and clamber up the steep steps of the central spire for a panoramic river view. Rest in a breezy riverside pavilion before taking the ferry back to Tha Tien. Get some refreshment at **Supanniga** *(see p75)*, just around the corner, then take an express boat to Phra Pinklao pier, which is a ten-minute walk from the **Royal Barge Museum** *(see p21)*: head up the road and take the first left down Soi Wat Dusitaram. Marvel over the intricate decoration of the vessels on display here before ⓞ heading back to your base.

See map on pp94–5 ←

The Best of the Rest

1 Christian Churches
MAP S5 ▪ S of Ratchawithi Road

Near the riverbank in Dusit district are three churches built for resident foreigners: St. Francis Xavier Church with its mainly Vietnamese congregation, the Church of the Immaculate Conception, which was established by French missionaries, and a small Cambodian church.

Mural at Wat Suwannaram

2 Wat Suwannaram
MAP S5 ▪ 33 Soi 32, Charan Sanit Wong Road ▪ 02 433 8045 ▪ Open 8am–5pm daily

This temple is home to superb murals depicting episodes from the *Jataka* tales, which tell the story of the Buddha's previous lives.

3 Wat Indrawiharn
MAP D1 ▪ 144 Wisut Kasat Road ▪ 02 281 1406 ▪ Open 6am–6pm daily

The main attraction of this temple tucked away in the backstreets of Dusit is the 105-ft (32-m) tall standing Buddha.

4 Wat Kalayanamit
MAP B6 ▪ Soi 6, Arun Amarin Road ▪ Open 8am–5pm daily

The country's largest indoor sitting Buddha (50 ft/15 m) and its biggest bronze bell are both found here.

5 Wat Prayun
MAP C6 ▪ Pratchatipok Road ▪ Open 8am–6pm daily

An artificial hill covered with *chedis* (stupas) and shrines is the highlight at Wat Prayun's cemetery. Devotees release turtles in the pond nearby.

6 Church of Santa Cruz
MAP C6 ▪ Soi Kudi Chin ▪ Open 5–8pm Mon–Sat & 9am–8pm Sun

Established by the Portuguese in 1770, this church's building dates back to 1913. It is now pastel in color and has an octagonal dome.

7 Wat Rakhang
MAP A4 ▪ Soi Wat Rakhang

This temple has a wooden scripture library behind the *bot* (ordination hall), where there are murals from the days when Rama I (r.1782–1809) lived here as a monk.

8 Thewet Flower Market
MAP D1 ▪ Krung Kasem Road ▪ Open 9am–6pm daily

With its bright blooms, sweet scent in the air, and the friendly vendors, this canalside market is good to explore.

9 Prasart Museum
MAP U6 ▪ 9 Krungthep Kreetha Soi 4A ▪ 02 379 3601 ▪ Open 9:30am–2pm Tue–Sun (by appointment) ▪ Adm

Set in a landscaped garden, this museum features artworks housed in reproductions of famous buildings.

10 Bangkok Dolls Museum
MAP T5 ▪ 85 Soi Mo Leng, Ratchaprarop Road ▪ 02 245 3008 ▪ Open 8am–5pm Tue–Sat ▪ www.bangkokdolls.com

This museum *(see p51)* displays dolls from around the world.

Restaurants

PRICE CATEGORIES
For a meal for one with one or two dishes
and a soft drink, including service.

B under B200 **BB** B200–1,000
BBB over B1,000

1 Madam Saranair
MAP T6 ▪ 139/1 Sukhumvit Soi
21 ▪ 02 61 7984 ▪ Open 8am–10pm
Mon–Fri, 11am–8pm Sat & Sun ▪ BB
Expect traditional Thai food at this
friendly, informal restaurant; the
tom yum soup is particularly popular.

2 Le Dalat
MAP T6 ▪ 57 Sukhumvit Soi
23 (Soi Prasanmitr) ▪ 02 259 9593
▪ Open 11:30am–2:30pm & 5:30–
10pm daily ▪ BB
Bangkok's top Vietnamese restaurant
serves diners a host of exquisitely
prepared traditional dishes.

3 Blue Elephant
MAP N6 ▪ 233 South Sathorn
Road ▪ 02 673 9353–8 ▪ Open
11:30am–2:30pm & 6–10:30pm daily
▪ www.blueelephant.com ▪ BBB
Set in a stunning century-old
building, the Blue Elephant specializes in Royal Thai cuisine.

4 Rendez-vous au Lys
MAP T6 ▪ 148/11 Nang
Linchi Soi 6 ▪ 02 077
5453 ▪ Open 11am–
2:30pm & 5:30–11pm
Mon, Tue, & Thu–
Sat, 11am–11pm
Sun ▪ BB
This garden restaurant
serves traditional French cuisine,
including good-value set lunches.

Thai food at Celadon

5 Cabbages & Condoms
MAP T6 ▪ 10 Sukhumvit Soi 12
▪ 02 229 4610 ▪ Open 11am–10:30pm
daily ▪ BB
Reasonable prices make this place
a good choice, and all proceeds go
toward AIDS prevention programs.

6 Baan Khanitha
MAP T6 ▪ 69 South Sathorn
Road ▪ 02 675 4200–1 ▪ Open
11am–11pm daily ▪ www.baan-
khanitha.com ▪ BB
One of the city's oldest upscale restaurants serving classic Thai dishes.

Upmarket restaurant Baan Khanitha

7 Indus
MAP T6 ▪ 71 Sukhumvit Soi
26 ▪ Open 11am–3pm & 5–11pm
Mon–Thu, 11am–11pm Fri–Sun
▪ www.indusbangkok.com ▪ BB
Indus serves contemporary Indian
vegetarian and meat dishes.

8 Celadon
MAP Q5 ▪ Sukhothai Hotel,
13/3 South Sathorn Road ▪ 02 344
8888 ▪ Open noon–2pm &
6–10pm daily ▪ BBB
This award-winning restaurant
serves sublime Thai food.

9 Supatra River House
MAP A4 ▪ 266 Soi Wat
Rakhang ▪ 02 411 0305
▪ Open 11:30am–2:30pm
& 5:30–10pm daily ▪ BB
Excellent seafood and
great riverside views at this restaurant.

10 Basil
MAP T6 ▪ Sheraton Grande
Sukhumvit, 250 Sukhumvit Road
▪ 02 649 8366 ▪ Open noon–2:30pm
& 6–10:30pm Mon–Fri & Sun,
6–10:30pm Sat ▪ BB
Diners can savor delicious Thai
dishes in sophisticated surroundings.

See map on pp94–5

Bars and Pubs

① Mikkeller Bangkok
MAP T6 ▪ 26 Yaek 2, Soi 10, Soi Ekamai, Sukhumvit Road ▪ 02 381 9891 ▪ Open 5pm–midnight daily

Located in a suburban house, this branch of the famous Danish micro-brewery offers 30 craft beers from around the world on tap.

② Iron Balls
MAP T6 ▪ Park Lane shopping mall, Sukhumvit Soi 63 ▪ Open 2pm–midnight daily

Relax amid the wrought ironwork in a leather armchair, sipping a delicious Negroni that's made with gin from the on-site micro-distillery.

Stunning skyline views at Octave

③ Octave Rooftop Lounge Bar
MAP T6 ▪ Marriott Sukhumvit, 45th floor, Sukhumvit Soi 57 ▪ 02 797 0000 ▪ Open 5pm–2am daily

One of the best rooftop bars in the city, with 360-degree views, Octave is perfect for a sunset drink before dinner and clubbing on Soi Thonglor.

④ Rendezvous
MAP T6 ▪ 138 Sukhumvit Road ▪ 02 254 0404 ▪ Open 8am–10pm daily

A marble bar is the centerpiece at this stylish establishment in the Landmark Hotel – a classy alternative on the boisterous Sukhumvit Road.

⑤ Zanzibar
MAP T6 ▪ 139 Sukhumvit Soi 11 ▪ 02 651 2900 ▪ Open 9am–2am daily

Set in a lovely garden, this Italian bar and restaurant has been a hit since day one. There is a live jazz band here every night.

⑥ Tensui
MAP T6 ▪ 33 Sukhumvit Soi 16 ▪ 02 663 2281 ▪ Open 11:30am–2pm & 5:30–10pm daily

An elegant restaurant serving fine sake and exquisitely prepared traditional Japanese cuisine.

⑦ Tuba
MAP T6 ▪ 30 Soi 21, Sukhumvit Road, Soi 63 ▪ 02 711 5500 ▪ Open 9am–midnight daily

A second-hand furniture shop and restaurant by day; by night a place to play pool and listen to some 70s tunes.

⑧ Black Swan
MAP T6 ▪ Sukhumvit Soi 19 ▪ 02 253 5141 ▪ Open 8am–1am daily

As the name suggests, this is a British-style pub offering a range of imported beers and generous portions of typical pub food.

⑨ Brewski
MAP T6 ▪ Radisson Blu Plaza Hotel, Sukhumvit Road ▪ 02 302 3333 ▪ Open 5pm–1am daily

This panoramic rooftop bar offers 18 craft beers and ciders on tap, plus a 100 more in bottles.

⑩ WTF
MAP T6 ▪ 7 Soi 51, Sukhumvit Road ▪ 02 662 6246 ▪ Open 5pm–1am Tue–Sun

A cool, Spanish-influenced bar that doubles as an art gallery, WTF offers great tapas, cocktails, and wines.

Nightclubs and Entertainment

Elaborate dance performance at Calypso Cabaret

1 Calypso Cabaret
MAP S6 ▪ Asiatique the Riverfront, 2194 Charoen Krung 72–76 Road ▪ 02 688 1415 ▪ Show 7:30 & 9pm daily ▪ Adm ▪ www. calypsocabaret.com

Thailand's most famous cabaret show is a riot of sequins, song, and dance *(see p55)*.

2 Glow
MAP T6 ▪ 96/4–5 Sukhumvit Soi 23 ▪ Open 9:30pm–3am Wed–Sun

International DJs play mostly house and techno here.

3 Bluebird Jazz Bar
MAP T6 ▪ 355/3 Thong Lo Road ▪ 089 777 9248 ▪ Open 5–11pm Wed–Sun

It feels like you're in the performers' living room at this cozy jazz bar, which features live music five nights a week.

4 Studio Lam
MAP T6 ▪ Soi 51, Sukhumvit Road ▪ 02 261 6661 ▪ Open 6pm–2am Tue–Sun

DJs play great Thai folk music every night at this friendly neighborhood bar.

5 Tawandang German Brewery
MAP T6 ▪ 462/61 Narathiwat Ratchanakharin ▪ 02 678 1114–5 ▪ Open 5pm–1am daily

Get a big helping of home-brewed beer while big bands play *morlam* music from northeast Thailand.

6 Lumphini Boxing Stadium
MAP T4 ▪ 6 Ram Intra Road near Don Muang Airport ▪ 06 2639 5596 ▪ Bouts: 7pm Tue & Fri, 4 & 8:10pm Sat ▪ Adm ▪ www.lumpineemuaythai.com

Bangkok's second major Thai boxing stadium *(see p55)*.

7 Hair of the Dog
MAP T6 ▪ 27 Sukhumvit Road ▪ Open 11am–midnight daily ▪ www.hairofthedogbkk.com

A great selection of beers, bottled and on tap, from some of the best craft beer brewers in Bangkok.

8 Living Room
MAP T6 ▪ Sheraton Grande Sukhumvit, 250 Sukhumvit Road ▪ 02 649 8888 ▪ Open 9am–midnight daily

A stylish hang-out, Living Room features top jazz musicians every evening and at Sunday lunch.

9 Fat Gutz Saloon
MAP U5 ▪ Central Eastville, Chalong Rat Expressway ▪ 06 3901 1115 ▪ Open 10:30am–1am daily

This place has a chic, upmarket clientele, who come for the fish and chips, and live blues performances.

10 Muangthai Rachadalai Theatre
MAP T5 ▪ 99 Ratchadaphisek Road ▪ Adm ▪ www.rachadalai.com

Hosts touring productions and Thai music and dance shows.

See map on pp94–5 ⇐

🔟 Beyond Bangkok

Bangkok's sights are liable to cause sensory overload, from the dazzling temples to the constant crowds. Fortunately, when visitors feel they need a break, there are plenty of opportunities for a day trip or an overnight stay away from the city. Tour operators can arrange undemanding and entertaining trips to nearby attractions, such as the Floating Market and the Muang Boran (Ancient City). Those who want to travel further afield can head for the ruins of Ayutthaya, the country's ancient capital, or Kanchanaburi, where a bridge over the Kwai River and a number of World War II-era Allied cemeteries can be found. If it is tropical beaches you long for, make for Pattaya, or Koh Samed with its powder-soft sands.

A monkey at Khao Yai

BEYOND BANGKOK

① Top 10 Sights
see pp102–05

1 Koh Si Chang
MAP U3 ▪ 62 miles (99 km) SE of Bangkok

Rarely visited by foreigners, this small, rocky island is located 5 miles (8 km) off the east Gulf coast. It has a selection of everything – secluded beaches with clear waters, a hilly interior ripe for exploring, and the remains of Rama V's palace, plus some reasonable accommodations. The most popular beach on the island is Tham Phang Beach.

2 Bang Pa-In
While visiting Ayutthaya, it is well worth stopping off at the nearby royal retreat of Bang Pa-In. Established by King Prasat Thong (r.1629–56) in the mid-17th century and rebuilt by Rama IV and Rama V (see p38), its exuberant buildings are an eclectic mix of Thai architecture, particularly in the Aisawan Thipphaya-at (see p34) pavilion, and European influences, as seen in the Phra Thinang Warophat Phiman. The manicured lawns and tranquil lakes give the place a relaxed feel.

3 Damnoen Saduak Floating Market

Although this floating market (see pp24–5) is considered by some to be nothing more than a show put on for tourists, it is certainly the best example of its kind. The market gives an idea of how life in this region once revolved around small boats plying their trade on narrow canals. Arrive early (or even better, stay overnight) to avoid the crowds emerging from tour buses at around 10am, and you will be rewarded with lively scenes of locals in traditional wear, *sampans* (flat-bottomed boats) piled high with appetizing fruits, and bowls of noodles served directly from floating kitchens.

Damnoen Saduak Floating Market

4 Muang Boran (Ancient City)
MAP T2 ▪ 20 miles (33 km) from Bangkok on Sukhumvit Road, Bangpoo ▪ 02 026 8800 ▪ Open 9am–6pm daily ▪ Adm ▪ www. muangboranmuseum.com

Covering a huge area designed in the shape of Thailand, this cultural park contains reconstructions of some of the country's most famous temples and monuments. It may sound like a tacky theme park, but the site offers a visually impressive and informative experience. Visitors can explore the site by car, tram, or bicycle, and it is rarely crowded.

Lakeside pavilion at Muang Boran (Ancient City)

5 Khao Yai
MAP U1 ▪ 105 miles (170 km) NE of Bangkok

Thailand's first National Park, this mountainous, forested area is home to elephants, tigers, and gibbons, plus over 300 species of birds. There are several waterfalls and bat caves, as well as resorts and golf courses in the foothills outside the park's boundaries. Trekking and mountain biking tours are offered, as well as camping. Visitors should plan on spending the night here to fully appreciate this natural wonderland.

6 Koh Samed
MAP U3 ▪ 124 miles (200 km) SE of Bangkok

Easily the best beach escape from the capital, Koh Samed is an island with clear waters and fine sand, as well as a national park. Due to its popularity, accommodation rates have spiraled. By avoiding weekends and public holidays, it is possible to enjoy the idyllic surroundings without feeling like a sardine in a can.

Crystal-clear waters of Koh Samed

7 Hua Hin
MAP S3 ▪ 118 miles (190 km) SW of Bangkok

Thailand's oldest beach resort was popularized by the royal family when they had a summer palace built here in 1926. Though the 3-mile (5-km) beach is fine for a stroll or a pony ride, shade is limited, and the shallow bay can frustrate swimmers. Vestiges of the past remain in the train station and the squid piers along the front.

Ancient ruins at Ayutthaya

8 Ayutthaya
From 1350 to 1767, Ayutthaya ruled supreme as the capital of its own kingdom, only to be abandoned after being sacked by the Burmese (see p38). The Ayutthaya Historical Park features ancient ruins set in tranquil countryside. The main temples – Wat Ratchaburana, Wat Mahathat, and Wat Sri Sanphet (see pp32–5) – can be covered in a day trip.

9 Pattaya
MAP U3 ▪ 91 miles (147 km) SE of Bangkok

Pattaya is infamous for its go-go bars, discos, cabarets, and countless "bar beers" – open-sided bars with friendly hostesses. The town also features a number of family attractions, such as Pattaya Park Water Park, Mini Siam, Underwater World, and the Art in Paradise museum. Watersports and golf are also big here, and there

---

THE DEATH RAILWAY

Between 1942–3, about 16,000 Allied prisoners of war and 90,000 Asians died during the construction of a railroad line from Thailand to Burma. The Japanese saw the line as crucial to their occupation of Southeast Asia. After the Japanese surrender, the British tore up the track. The rail link was never re-established.

are some excellent seafood restaurants and well-stocked shopping malls.

⑩ Kanchanaburi
MAP S2 ▪ 80 miles (130 km) W of Bangkok

At the western edge of the Central Plains, Kanchanaburi is a popular day trip from Bangkok. The main sights are the bridge over the Kwai River and the war cemeteries where thousands of allied soldiers who died in World War II during the construction of the "Death Railway" to Burma are buried. The Thailand-Burma Railway Center explains how the disastrous events unfolded. Kanchanaburi is also the jumping-off point for several natural sites, including the Erawan National Park, with its waterfalls.

Waterfalls near Kanchanaburi

▶ MORNING

Start the day relaxing on Jomtien Beach, on the endless stretch of sand just south of **Pattaya** town center. Take a swim to cool down or if you are feeling energetic have a go at waterskiing, wind-surfing, or parasailing. If you haven't been snacking all morning on seafood or fruit sold by wandering vendors on the beach, head for **Big Kahuna** (Map U3; Tabphaya Road; 097 242 232; open 7:30am–8pm daily) near the north end of the beach for hearty hamburgers and Cuban sandwiches.

AFTERNOON

After lunch, head up to Khao Phra Tamnak from where there are excellent views of Pattaya Beach. Next, head north of town to the Sanctuary of Truth, a fabulous palace that blends influences from Khmer, Hindu, and Buddhist architecture. Finish the afternoon's sightseeing with a visit to **Mini Siam**, which features miniature models of some of the country's most famous buildings.

NIGHT

Begin your evening in any of the beachfront beer bars, to get a feel for the party mood of the town. For dinner, go to **PIC Kitchen** (Map U3; Soi 5; 03 842 8374; open 11am–2pm & 5pm–midnight daily) and indulge in a delicious curry. Next, check out a Thai cabaret at Tiffany's. After the show, either head for bed or explore Pattaya's pulsating nightlife.

See map on p102 ←

Streetsmart

**Preparing and selling boat noodles
at a floating market in Bangkok**

Getting Around

Arriving by Air

Most travelers to Bangkok arrive by air, unless entering Thailand via a land crossing from Malaysia, Cambodia, Laos, or Myanmar. The city's airport **Suvarnabhumi International Airport (BKK)** hosts over 80 airlines with direct flights from most major cities. There is one terminal operating international and domestic flights, with arrivals on Level 2 and departures on Level 4. The airport is around 16 miles (25 km) east of Bangkok.

North of Bangkok is the other international airport, **Don Muang International Airport (DMK)**. It operates domestic and international low-cost airlines such as Nok Air, Air Asia, and Thai Lion Air. Thai Airways has an extensive network of budget flights within Thailand and to destinations in Southeast Asia.

The Suvarnabhumi Airport Rail Link (SARL) leaves from the basement of the airport terminal and transfers into the city; tickets are very affordable. It also connects with Bangkok's two MRT (mass rapid transit) systems: the Skytrain and the subway.

Metered taxis from both airports charge a B50 pick-up fee. There are tolls to pay on the overhead expressways as well.

International Train Travel

It is possible to reach Bangkok from Singapore and Malaysia by train.

Most trains terminate at **Bang Sue Grand Station**. Trains from Kanchanaburi, and some from Hua Hin, terminate at **Thonburi Station**.

Long-Distance Bus Travel

Thailand offers overland itineraries that include visits to neighboring countries. Buses from Malaysia terminate at the **Eastern Bus Terminal**, while those from Cambodia and Laos arrive at the **Northern Bus Terminal** at Mochit.

All vehicles are air-conditioned, with a toilet, reclining seats, and plenty of leg room. It's best to book in advance at peak periods, but otherwise you can just turn up at the coach station at least half an hour before departure.

Rapid Transit Systems

Bangkok has two urban mass transit systems, the **Skytrain (BTS)** and the **MRT**, a subway. The Skytrain is an elevated railway with two lines. The Sukhumvit Line runs from Chatuchak Weekend Market, through the downtown area at Rama I and Ploenchit roads, along Sukhumvit Road to Soi Thonglor, and into the eastern suburbs. The Silom Line runs from the National Stadium (near Jim Thompson House), through the downtown Silom area, to Saphan Thaksin (good for accessing river boats), and into Thonburi. The two lines intersect at Siam Square.

It gets busy during rush hours (7am to 9am and 5pm to 7pm). To avoid lines at the ticket vending machines, go to the manned ticket counters and buy a one-day pass for B140 (unlimited trips) or a Rabbit Card (stored-value card) for B200. The last train is at midnight.

The MRT system's main Blue Line covers a 12-mile (20-km) underground loop from Hua Lampong Station, passing through Silom and Sukhumvit areas, and continuing to Chatuchak Weekend Market. Extension work was completed in 2020 and the extended route now connects Hua Lampong with Chinatown and the Old City.

The MRT intersects with the Skytrain at three stations. Transferring between them requires buying a new ticket. The MRT offers day passes and stored-value cards. Like the Skytrain, it gets busy during rush hours. The last train is at midnight.

Boats

Chao Phraya and **Khlong Saen Saeb** express boat services *(see p21)* are good for sightseeing and transportation, especially to go from Downtown to the Old City until the new MRT stations open. Hotels on the Thonburi side offer free shuttles. Chartering a longtail boat is an option.

Buses

BMTA runs an extensive bus network with very cheap fares. Most routes operate from 4am to

10pm, with a few providing a 24-hour service. Buses can get stuck in heavy traffic, so it is best to book an air-conditioned bus.

Car Rental

Driving in Bangkok is not recommended. Those who wish to travel by car usually hire a driver with detailed local road knowledge. Car rental companies such as **Hertz** and **Budget** offer drivers.

Taxis

Metered taxis are easy to find and relatively cheap, with a flag fare of B35 for the first 0.6 miles (1 km) and B5.5 for every 0.6 mile (1 km) after that. The meter also calculates time, charging for slow-moving traffic. A short journey costs about B60. Insist on using the meter, since it is cheaper than negotiating a fare. App-based taxi services such as **InDriver** (uses standard Thai taxis) and **Grab** (choice of vehicle) operate in Bangkok.

Motorbike Taxi

Motorbike taxi riders wait on the corners of important roads. They are useful for routes that cannot be covered by other modes of transport. Fares are negotiable, starting at B20 for a short trip. They are fast and can squeeze through traffic, but are not recommended for children.

Cycling

Bike-shares and rentals exist in Bangkok, and the Old City has dedicated bike lanes. It's best to start with a cycling tour. Try **Follow Me**, **Pun Pun Bike Share**, or **Spice Roads**.

Tuk-Tuk

A ride in a tuk-tuk is an essential part of the Thai experience, and it can be exciting weaving through traffic in these open-sided three-wheelers. However, they are noisy and unprotected from pollution. Fares must be negotiated before you start.

Walking

Visitors can experience the vibrant day-to-day life and culture of Bangkok by walking around the city. The key to a pleasant walk is to avoid major thoroughfares and walk in the quiet *sois* (lanes) that run parallel to the main roads. Use a good street map to plot your route via the *sois*. Guided walking tours also take place around the city.

DIRECTORY

ARRIVING BY AIR

Don Muang International Airport (DMK)
w donmueangairport.com

Suvarnabhumi International Airport (BKK)
w suvarnabhumi.airportthai.co.th

INTERNATIONAL TRAIN TRAVEL

Bang Sue Grand Station
MAP T5 ▪ Thoet Damri Rd 📞 02 587 4613

Thonburi Station
MAP A3 ▪ Siriraj, Bangkok Noi

LONG-DISTANCE BUS TRAVEL

Northern Bus Terminal
MAP T5 ▪ Phahonyothin Rd 📞 02 272 0299

Eastern Bus Terminal
MAP S5 ▪ Sukhumvit Rd, Phra Khanong 📞 02 391 2504

RAPID TRANSIT SYSTEMS

MRT
w bemplc.co.th

Skytrain (BTS)
w bts.co.th

BOATS

Chao Phraya
w chaophrayaexpressboat.com

Khlong Saen Saeb
w khlongsaensaep.com

BUSES

BMTA
w bmta.co.th

CAR RENTAL

Budget
w budget.co.th

Hertz
w hertzthailand.com

TAXIS

Grab
w grab.com

InDriver
w indriver.com

CYCLING

Follow Me
w followmebiketour.com

Pun Pun Bike Share
w punpunbikeshare.com

Spice Roads
w spiceroads.com

Practical Information

Passports and Visas

For entry requirements, including visas, consult your nearest Thai embassy or check the **Thai Ministry of Foreign Affairs** website.

Visitors to Thailand must have a passport valid for at least six months from the date of entry. Most travelers, including citizens of the UK, US, Australia, and the EU, can enter Thailand for up to 30 days without a pre-arranged visa. For longer visits, apply at the nearest Thai embassy for a 60-day visa, which must be used within three months of issue. Non-immigrant 90-day visas are available if there is a good reason for extending a stay, such as education or business. Visas for 30 or 60 days can be extended by 30 days at the **Immigration Office** for a fee. If you overstay your visa, there is a B500 fine per day. These regulations can be subject to change.

Numerous countries, including Australia, the UK, and the US, have consular representation in the city.

Government Advice

Now more than ever, it is important to consult both your and the Thai government's advice before travelling. The **UK Foreign and Commonwealth Office**, the **US State Department**, the **Australian Department of Foreign Affairs and Trade**, and the **Royal Thai Government** offer the latest information on security, health, and local regulations.

Customs Information

You can find information on the laws relating to goods and currency taken in or out of Thailand on the **Thai Customs Department** website. There are strict regulations around the export of antiques and Buddha images.

Insurance

We recommend that you take out a comprehensive insurance policy covering theft, loss of belongings, medical care, cancellations and delays, and read the small print carefully.

Vaccinations

There are no legal immunization requirements unless you are traveling from a country known to be infected with yellow fever. However, it is a good idea to be immunized against polio, tetanus, typhoid, and hepatitis A.

BCG (tuberculosis), hepatitis B, rabies, diphtheria, and Japanese encephalitis vaccinations are recommended for people visiting rural areas. Check the latest vaccination requirements with your doctor 4–6 weeks before traveling.

For information regarding COVID-19 vaccination requirements, consult government advice.

Health

There are several public and private hospitals in Bangkok, and highly qualified doctors who speak good medical English. Healthcare is affordable in Thailand, and the country is popular for medical tourism. **Bangkok Nursing Home (BNH) Hospital** and **Bumrungrad Hospital** are good for serious issues and surgery. In an emergency, call the **Medical Hotline**.

For minor ailments, local clinics are reliable, and staff often speak some English. Pharmacies are usually well stocked. Prescriptions are not required for antibiotics. Nonetheless, if you require a specific medication, bring a supply with you, with prescription labels.

Those in need of dental care can visit places such as the **Dental Hospital** which offers professional and affordable care.

Stomach upsets caused by unfamiliarity with the food or contaminated water, are common. Choose food stalls that are popular with locals.

Acclimatization to the sometimes oppressive humidity and heat of Thailand can often take longer than expected. It is wise to drink plenty of bottled water, rest in the shade, and avoid the midday sun for the first few days.

Smoking, Alcohol, and Drugs

Smoking is officially prohibited in indoor public areas, although some restaurants and bars do have designated areas for smoking indoors. Importation or sale of e-cigarettes is illegal. Thailand has a limit of 0.50mg/l of alcohol when driving, and fines for crossing the limit can be high.

Possession of illegal drugs, including cannabis, can risk a long prison sentence in Thailand.

ID

By law you must carry photo identification at all times. A photocopy of your passport photo page and visa page is acceptable and means you can leave your passport in your hotel's safe.

Personal Security

Though traveling in Thailand is generally safe, there are some precautions that should be followed. Bag-snatching from passing motorcycles and pick-pocketing are common in Bangkok, so it's best to avoid carrying large sums of money or wearing much jewelry. It is advisable to leave your passport and valuables in your hotel's safe. Avoid touts and other hustlers. The area outside the Grand Palace is notorious for touts.

In case of emergency contact the **Tourist Police**, which has an English-speaking operator. Lines are open from 8am to midnight. The Tourist Police also have a website. The **Metropolitan Mobile Police** covers general emergencies in the city.

Homosexuality was made legal in Thailand in 1956 and while the LGBTQ+ community is generally accepted, the law does not yet recognize same-sex marriages or civil unions. There is a vibrant LGBTQ+ scene in Bangkok, but areas outside the major urban centers may be more conservative. **Utopia Asia** is a good source of information for LGBTQ+ travelers visiting Thailand.

Travelers with Specific Requirements

Facilities for visitors with specific requirements are generally good in Bangkok. Every MRT station in the city has lifts and wheelchair access. Neither trains nor buses are fully accessible however, so hiring a car and driver is usually the best option. Pavements across the city can also be uneven and lacking in ramps. Many high-end hotels in the capital and major tourist areas are also well-equipped to accommodate those with specific requirements. Facilities for wheelchair-users outside of the city are limited. There are also few audio signals for visually-impaired travelers at traffic crossings in the city.

Access the World and the **Tourism Authority of Thailand** have advice and information.

DIRECTORY

PASSPORTS AND VISAS

Immigration Office
w bangkok.immigration.go.th

Thai Ministry of Foreign Affairs
w mfa.go.th

GOVERNMENT ADVICE

Australian Department of Foreign Affairs and Trade
w smartraveller.gov.au

Royal Thai Government
w thaigov.go.th

UK Foreign and Commonwealth Office
w gov.uk/foreign-travel-advice

US State Department
w travel.state.gov

CUSTOMS INFORMATION

Thai Customs Department
w customs.go.th

HEALTH

BNH Hospital
w bnhhospital.com

Bumrungrad Hospital
c 2 066 8888
w bumrungrad.com

Dental Hospital
c 2 092 2000
w dentalhospitalbangkok.com

Medical Hotline
c 1669

PERSONAL SECURITY

Metropolitan Mobile Police
c 191

Tourist Police
c 1155
w touristpolice.go.th

Utopia Asia
w utopia-asia.com

TRAVELERS WITH SPECIFIC REQUIREMENTS

Access the World
w wheelchairtraveling.com

Tourism Authority of Thailand
Off MAP R2 ▪ 1600 Petchaburi Road
w tourismthailand.org

Time Zone

Thailand is 7 hours ahead of Greenwich Mean Time, 12 hours ahead of US Eastern Standard Time, and three hours behind Australian Eastern Standard Time.

Money

The official currency is the Thai baht. Foreign currency may be accepted, but the rate of exchange will not be favorable. Most establishments accept major credit, debit, and prepaid currency cards, though it is always a good idea to carry cash for small transactions.

Tipping is not customary in Thailand but a small tip as a mark of appreciation is welcome nonetheless. The following amounts are recommended as a guideline: 20 baht per person served in a restaurant; 20 baht per bag for a hotel porter; 100 baht for the concierge; round up taxi fares to the nearest 10 baht.

Electrical Appliances

The electrical current in Thailand flows at 220 volts AC, 50 Hz, and most plug sockets are of the two-pin variety. Adaptors are readily available in department stores.

Cell Phones and Wi-Fi

Thailand uses the GSM 4G cell phone and data system, which is available in Bangkok and most other cities and towns, and the populated islands. Free Wi-Fi is available in virtually all accommodations, as well as many restaurants, cafes, and malls. Alternatively, it is possible to buy a cell phone cheaply; prepaid SIM cards can be purchased in any convenience store.

Postal Services

Thailand has a reliable postal system, and stamps are available at all post offices and at many hotels. Letters and postcards usually take at least one week to reach Europe and North America. Post office hours are normally 8:30am to 4:30pm Monday to Friday and 9am to noon on Saturday. Packages should be sent by registered mail or via International Express Mail Service (EMS). DHL, FEDEX, and UPS are all available in large towns and cities.

Weather

The best time to visit is November to February, with clear skies and cooler temperatures, generally around 80° F (26.5° C). However, hotel rates tend to be higher, and tourist attractions more crowded. The hot season (March to May) is fine for a beach holiday but not for sightseeing. The rainy season (June to October) can be pleasant, and storms usually blow over quickly.

The tropical monsoon climate means that spring is hot, followed by summer rains. Loose, breathable layers are recommending when exploring the city. Bangkokians see short pants as beachwear, but visitors are given latitude, except in temples. During the rainy season umbrella vendors are everywhere.

Opening Hours

Most government offices are open from 8:30am to 4:30pm on weekdays, but many close for lunch. Tourist attractions tend to open from 9am to 5pm daily. Department stores open daily at 10am and close at 9 or 10pm. On public holidays, government offices, post offices, and banks are closed, but most shops, bars and restaurants remain open. The major national holiday is Songkran, in April, when much of Thailand closes for 3 to 7 days.

The COVID-19 pandemic proved that situations can change suddenly. Always check before visiting attractions and hospitality venues for up-to-date hours and booking requirements.

Visitor Information

The Tourism Authority of Thailand, the official government tourist board, has its headquarters in Bangkok. Its website provides comprehensive coverage of destinations and events, and maps and brochures are available from its office. There is also an app-based version of the website. The **Bangkok Tourism Division** is also a useful source of information and has booths around the city.

Local Customs

The people of Thailand are known for their tolerance, amiability, and helpfulness. Nonetheless, there are a few local values to bear in mind. Direct confrontation and aggressive behavior are considered particularly inappropriate. The monarchy, past and present, is protected by local reverence and the strict, draconian lèse-majesté laws, so avoid any mention of the royal family.

The head is considered a sacred part of the body, so do not touch people's heads, and avoid pointing your feet (which are considered lowly) at people or religious icons when seated.

Always remove your shoes when entering a home. Wearing ultrashort shorts, men going shirtless in public, and women going topless while at the beach are all considered impolite.

Visiting Buddhist Temples

Visitors are welcome in Thai wats, but should act and take photos respectfully, and dress modestly. Shorts and sleeveless shirts are not appropriate, and shoes should be removed before entering. Greet monks with a smile and a nod. Women are not permitted to hand anything directly to a monk.

Language

The official language in Thailand is Thai, but basic English is widespread, although not guaranteed. Cell phone apps offering voice to voice translation can come in handy.

Taxes and Refunds

Thailand imposes a 7 percent Value Added Tax (VAT) on goods and services. There is a VAT refund scheme for visitors who are in the country for less than 180 days. Look out for shops displaying a "VAT Refund for Tourists" sign. Each purchase must be to the value of at least 2,000 baht. Show your passport to the sales assistant who will fill out a VAT refund form, which you will need to present to the customs desk at the airport before departure.

Accommodation

In Bangkok, five-star accommodation can cost as little as a mid-range hotel in Europe or the US. For your money, you can expect a large room with a decent view, luxurious furnishings and decor, plenty of onsite bars and restaurants, and attentive hotel service.

Mid-range hotels offer all the basic comforts, like air-conditioned rooms, bathrooms with hot water, and television, though without the luxurious touches and elegance of top-end hotels. It is also well worth checking out the rapidly growing number of boutique hotels that offer a more personal touch and unique character, often missing even in top-end hotels.

Bangkok attracts a stream of budget tourists, mostly to Khao San Road. A typical cheap room here will be small, often without windows, with a bed, a fan, paper-thin walls, and shared bathrooms. The street is packed with lively bars and affordable dining options, but nearby areas are always worth exploring for quieter accommodations. The booking resource **Agoda** offers a range of budget hotels, as well as some higher range options.

It is a good idea to book your hotel room well in advance of your visit, especially if the hotel in question is highly rated, and even more so during the high season, from November to February or during major festivals. Internet booking services are useful, but be sure to check change and cancellation policies before booking. Some hotels offer good rates on their own websites.

Hotel rates hit a peak during the cool season (November to February), when many establishments operate at full occupancy. For the rest of the year, it is worth asking about discounts, especially if you plan to stay several nights.

Places to Stay

PRICE CATEGORIES

For a standard, double room per night (with breakfast if included), taxes and extra charges.

B under B1,800   **BB** B1,800–4,000   **BBB** over B4,000

Luxury Hotels

Anantara Bangkok Riverside Resort and Spa

MAP S6 ▪ 257 Charoen Nakhon Road, Thonburi ▪ 02 476 0022 ▪ www. anantara.com ▪ BBB
Built on prime property on the west bank of the Chao Phraya River, this huge complex has a lovely spa, fine gardens, many restaurants, and a pool. Each room has a private balcony.

Anantara Siam

MAP Q3 ▪ 55 Ratchadamri Road ▪ 02 126 8866 ▪ www.anantara.com ▪ BBB
Luxurious rooms, impeccable service, and a number of fine-dining restaurants make this one of Bangkok's best hotels. It is in an excellent location, with views over the green expanse of the Royal Bangkok Sports Club.

COMO Metropolitan Bangkok

MAP Q5 ▪ 27 South Sathorn Road ▪ 02 625 3333 ▪ www.comohotels. com ▪ BBB
Bangkok's trendiest hotel features a minimalist look and silk furnishings. Its two great restaurants, Nahm and Glow (see p101), and the members-only Met Bar attract the city's top design gurus.

Conrad Hotel

MAP R3 ▪ All Seasons Place, Withayu Road ▪ 02 690 9999 ▪ www. hilton.com ▪ BBB
Designed in contemporary Thai style, making lavish use of silk and wood, Conrad Hotel has lovely views over Lumphini Park (see p86). It has a central location, and its restaurants and bars are among the best in town.

Grand Hyatt Erawan Bangkok

MAP Q3 ▪ 494 Ratchadamri Road ▪ 02 254 1234 ▪ www. hyatt.com ▪ BBB
A grandiose entrance leads to guest rooms with large windows, marble baths, and trendy fittings. The afternoon tea in the Garden Lounge is a delight.

Mandarin Oriental Hotel

MAP M5 ▪ 48 Oriental Avenue ▪ 02 659 9000 ▪ www.mandarinoriental. com/bangkok ▪ BBB
The historic Oriental (see p85) has often been voted the world's best hotel for its superb facilities, exceptional views, and personalized service.

The Peninsula Hotel

MAP L5 ▪ 333 Charoen Nakhon Road ▪ 02 020 2888 ▪ www.peninsula. com ▪ BBB
The Peninsula has won several awards for its wave-shaped design and spacious guest rooms with fabulous views of the Chao Phraya River and the city. It has a three-tiered swimming pool, a gorgeous spa, and restaurants serving Thai, and Cantonese cuisine.

Royal Orchid Sheraton

MAP M4 ▪ 2 Captain Bush Lane ▪ 02 266 0123 ▪ www.marriott.com ▪ BBB
This 28-story hotel has pools and tennis courts, a fitness center and spa, restaurants serving royal Thai and Italian cuisine, and a relaxed riverside bar.

Shangri-La Hotel

MAP M6 ▪ 89 Soi Wat Suan Phlu, Charoen Krung Road ▪ 02 236 7777 ▪ www.shangri-la. com ▪ BBB
With 800 rooms, the riverside Shangri-La is one of Bangkok's biggest luxury hotels. It has several restaurants and bars; the excellent Chi, The Spa (see p44); a fitness center, pools, and tennis courts.

Siam Kempinski Hotel

MAP P2 ▪ 991/9 Rama I Road ▪ 02 162 9000 ▪ www.kempinski.com/ bangkok ▪ BBB
An Art Deco-inspired resort hotel in the heart of the city, the beautiful Siam Kempinski is set around a landscaped garden and has three pools. It also has a spa and an excellent contemporary Thai restaurant.

Sukhothai Hotel

MAP Q5 ▪ 13/3 South Sathorn Road ▪ 02 344 8888 ▪ www.sukhothai. com ▪ BBB

This hotel blends modern conveniences and traditional Thai architecture. Surrounded by lush gardens and pools, the hotel has luxurious rooms, three excellent restaurants, and a pool-terrace café.

W Hotel

MAP P6 ▪ 106 North Sathorn Road ▪ 02 344 4000 ▪ www.marriott. com ▪ BBB

Chic and sleek, this oasis of modern luxury also includes The House on Sathorn, a mansion that once housed the Russian Embassy, now a sumptuous restaurant and bar. Their Woo Bar is a Bangkok hot spot.

Business Hotels

Majestic Grande Sukhumvit

MAP T6 ▪ 12 Sukhumvit Soi 2 ▪ 02 262 2999 ▪ www.majesticgrande. com ▪ BB

Conveniently located, this opulent hotel offers an excellent range of facilities for business guests, including generous desk space in the rooms and a translation service in the business center.

InterContinental Hotel

MAP R3 ▪ 973 Ploenchit Road ▪ 02 656 0444 ▪ www.bangkok.inter continental.com ▪ BBB

Towering above Ploenchit's business district, this 37-story hotel is perfect for business travelers and shoppers, with the Skytrain

right at its doorstep. Huge rooms offer great views from the double-glazed, soundproofed windows.

Lebua at State Tower

MAP N5 ▪ 1055 Silom Road ▪ 02 624 9999 ▪ www.lebua.com ▪ BBB

This distinctive skyscraper with its golden dome is one of Bangkok's icons. It is also home to Breeze (see p91) and Sirocco, two of the city's top dining venues, as well as the stunning Sky Bar (see p92).

Marriott Marquis Queens Park

MAP T6 ▪ 199 Sukhumvit Soi 22 ▪ 02 059 5555 ▪ www.marriott.com ▪ BBB

The luxurious rooms at this hotel overlook Benjasiri Park. It has two swimming pools and also houses a spa. There are plenty of places to eat including a Thai–Western tea room, as well as a contemporary Asian restaurant on the rooftop.

Sheraton Grande Sukhumvit

MAP T6 ▪ 250 Sukhumvit Road ▪ 02 649 8888 ▪ www.sheratongrande sukhumvit.com ▪ BBB

Among Bangkok's best business hotels, the Sheraton Grande offers modern elegance with state-of-the-art facilities. Its business center is open 24 hours, and a footbridge connects the hotel to the Asoke Skytrain station.

Westin Grande Sukhumvit

MAP T6 ▪ 259 Sukhumvit Road ▪ 02 207 8000 ▪ www.marriott.com ▪ BBB

The rooms are designed with executive travelers in

mind, complete with soft beds and writing desks. The Vareena Spa and the Zest Bar and Terrace have panoramic views.

Mid-Range Hotels

Aloft Hotel Bangkok

MAP T6 ▪ 35 Sukhumvit Soi 11 ▪ 02 207 7000 ▪ www.marriott.com ▪ BB

Sheraton's mid-range chain provides trendy decor, large rooms, and efficient service. Levels (see p93), one of the city's hottest nightspots, is on the sixth floor. Soi 11 has many cafés and pubs.

Chillax Resort

MAP C2 ▪ 274 Samsen Road Soi 2 ▪ 02 629 4400 ▪ www.chillaxresort.com ▪ BB

This high-rise hotel has a rooftop infinity pool with incredible views over the city and the river. Each room has a Jacuzzi, good for unwinding after a long day's sightseeing.

Navalai River Resort

MAP C2 ▪ 45 Phra Athit Road ▪ 02 280 9955 ▪ www.navalai.com ▪ BB

Located on hip Phra Athit Road, near the Grand Palace, the Navalai has balconied rooms overlooking the Chao Phraya and a rooftop pool. There is also a riverside restaurant.

New Siam Riverside

MAP B2 ▪ 21 Phra Athit Road ▪ 02 629 3535 ▪ www.newsiam.net ▪ BB

This clean and quiet inn offers the best value rooms on the river in the lively Phra Athit area, near Khao San Road.

Rembrandt Hotel
MAP T6 ▪ 19 Sukhumvit Soi 18 ▪ 02 261 7100 ▪ www.rembrandt sukhumvit.com ▪ BB
In a quiet *soi* off the main Sukhumvit Road, near Soi Asok, the Rembrandt offers value well beyond its price and immaculate rooms, as well as the best Indian and Mexican restaurants in the city.

The Rose Hotel
MAP P5 ▪ 118 Surawong Road ▪ 02 266 8268 ▪ www.rosehotelbkk. com ▪ BB
Close to much of the Silom area's shopping and nightlife, the Rose offers comfortable, quiet rooms in contemporary Asian style. It has a swimming pool, an excellent restaurant, a gym, and a sauna.

Boutique Hotels

Luxx Hotel
MAP N5 ▪ 6/11 Decho Road ▪ 02 635 8800 ▪ www.staywithluxx. com ▪ BB
The minimalist appearance of the suites and compact rooms at this hotel will appeal to the young, hip, and trendy; and the location, just a few steps from the shops and nightlife of Silom Road, could not be better.

Shanghai Mansion
MAP L3 ▪ 479–81 Yaowarat Road ▪ 02 221 2121 ▪ www.shanghai mansion.com ▪ BB
In the heart of Chinatown, this chic and unusual hotel has just over 50 smallish rooms fitted with four-poster beds and painted in vibrant colors. Some are windowless.

There is a restaurant, massage/spa facilities, and a shuttle tuk-tuk service for guests.

Siam Heritage
MAP P5 ▪ 115/1 Surawong Road ▪ 02 353 6166 ▪ www.thesiamheritage. com ▪ BB
The rooms of this hotel are decorated in Northern and Central Thai style, with polished wood floors and antique-style furnishings. Services include a spa, a bakery, and a Thai restaurant.

AriyasomVilla Boutique Hotel
MAP T6 ▪ 65 Sukhumvit Soi 1 ▪ 02 254 8880 ▪ www. ariyasom.com ▪ BBB
This 1940s mansion is a serene urban oasis close to the Saen Saeb canal and downtown shopping areas. There's a lovely garden and pool, and great vegetarian food.

Chakrabongse Villas
MAP B5 ▪ 396 Maharaj Road ▪ 02 222 1290 ▪ www.thaivillas.com ▪ BBB
Located on the Chao Phraya River, near Wat Pho and with amazing views of Wat Arun, this stunning hotel comprises seven rooms and suites set in lush tropical gardens, with a pool and riverside dining terrace.

Praya Palazzo
MAP B2 ▪ 757/1 Somdet Phra Pin Klao Road, Soi 2 ▪ 02 883 2998 ▪ www. prayapalazzo.com ▪ BBB
With a riverfront location on the Thonburi side, this restored Italianate mansion is beautifully decorated and serves excellent Thai and Western food.

The Siam
MAP S5 ▪ 3/2 Khao Road, behind Vachira Hospital ▪ 02 206 6999 ▪ www.thesiam hotel.com ▪ BBB
Bangkok's top-rated small hotel, located in the quiet Dusit area, has 39 sumptuously decorated suites and villas with antique furniture and lovely views of the river.

Budget

A-One Inn
MAP P2 ▪ 25/13 Soi Kasemsan 1, Rama I Road ▪ 02 215 3029 ▪ www.aoneinn.com ▪ B
Tucked just around the corner from Siam Square, the shoppers' paradise, this upscale guesthouse has basic but clean rooms. The staff are friendly, there is Wi-Fi throughout, and it is only a few steps from the National Stadium BTS station.

iCheck Inn
MAP R3 ▪ 71 Sukhumvit Soi 2 ▪ 02 656 9877 ▪ www.icheckinn.com ▪ B
Part of a reliable chain of inns, this modest tower-block hotel features basic but comfortable rooms with corner sofas. It's located near several major embassies and shopping malls.

New Siam 2
MAP B2 ▪ 50 Trok Rong Mai, Phra Athit Road ▪ 02 629 0101 ▪ www.newsiam.net ▪ B
This modern budget hotel offers peace and privacy near the Grand

Palace. Rooms are well equipped with in-room safes and private bathrooms, while air-conditioning costs extra. There is a small swimming pool.

Riverview Guesthouse

MAP E6 ▪ 768 Songwat Road ▪ 02 234 5429 ▪ www.riverviewbkk. com ▪ B

Located in a backstreet beside the San Jao Sien Khong temple in Chinatown, this family-run guesthouse has refurbished rooms and good views of the Chao Phraya River from the upper floors. There is a great rooftop bar and restaurant.

For You Residence

MAP N5 ▪ 839 Silom Road ▪ 02 635 3900 ▪ www.foryouresidence. com ▪ B

This comfortable hotel offers bright, well-lit rooms – with a simple, pine-rich aesthetic – and decent international breakfasts. Happy hour at the bar is 5–7pm and there's an on-site convenience store, too.

Wall Street Inn

MAP P5 ▪ 37/20–24 Surawong Road ▪ 02 233 4144 ▪ www.wall streetinnhotel.com ▪ B

The smartly furnished rooms in this hotel come with comfortable beds, cable TV, and minibars. There is also a business center, a coffee shop, and a massage parlor offering traditional massage and foot reflexology.

Beyond Bangkok

Away Kanchanaburi Dheva Mantra Resort & Spa

MAP S2 ▪ Moo 3, Thamakham Road, Kanchanaburi ▪ 034 615 999 ▪ www.dheva mantraresort.com ▪ BB

The sumptuous rooms here are set in an elegant building and surrounded by huge gardens. Although it is a bit out of town, there are some lovely views over the river and mountains. There's also a great spa.

Bangkok Tree House

MAP T6 ▪ 60 Moo 1, Petch Cha Hueng Road, Bang Namphueng ▪ 08 2995 1150 ▪ www.bangkok treehouse.com ▪ BB

A boutique eco-resort located in Bang Krajao, Bangkok's green lung (see p49), the Tree House is accessible only by boat or on foot. So close yet so different from the metropolis, it offers organic food and free bicycles – ideal for exploring this rural area.

Kantary Hotel

MAP T1 ▪ 168 Moo 1, Rojana Road, Ayutthaya ▪ 035 337 177 ▪ www. kantaryhouse-bangkok. com ▪ BB

This is the best choice for an overnight's stay in Ayutthaya. A great-value stylish hotel with ideal suites for families, it also has a swimming pool, Jacuzzi, and sauna.

Avani Hua Hin Resort and Villas

MAP S3 ▪ 1499 Phetkasem Road, Hua Hin ▪ 032 898 989 ▪ www. avanihotels.com ▪ BBB

Set around landscaped gardens and three

expansive swimming pools, this chic hotel offers a variety of rooms – including pool villas and some with Jacuzzis on their balconies. There is also a contemporary spa and a fine Italian beach-front restaurant.

Hilton Hua Hin Resort & Spa

MAP S3 ▪ 33 Nares Damri Road, Hua Hin ▪ 032 538 999 ▪ www3. hilton.com ▪ BBB

There may be newer and more spectacular hotels in Hua Hin, but the Hilton is within walking distance of old Hua Hin and the Night Market. It also fronts onto a beautiful beach, and its top-floor restaurant is one of the best in town.

Novotel Suvarnabhumi Airport Hotel

MAP T2 ▪ Next to the airport terminal and SARL station ▪ 02 131 1111 ▪ www.novotel airportbkk.com ▪ BBB

If an airport hotel is needed, this is by far the best. The rooms are very elegant, and there is an excellent spa. Enjoy a relaxing atmosphere, and good food at any of the five restaurants and cafés situated just off the atrium lobby.

Sugar Hut

MAP U3 ▪ 391/38 Moo 10, Pattaya Na Jomtien Road, Pattaya ▪ 038 251 686 ▪ www.sugarhut resort.com ▪ BBB

Stay here for elegant Thai-style villas beyond the busy part of town, with superb gardens, Jacuzzi, a pool, and delicious Thai food.

For a key to hotel price categories see p114

General Index

Acknowledgments

This edition updated by

Contributor Daniel Stables

Senior Editor Alison McGill

Senior Designer Stuti Tiwari

Project Editors Parnika Bagla, Lucy Sara-Kelly

Editor Mark Silas

Project Art Editor Ankita Sharma

Picture Research Administrator Vagisha Pushp

Picture Research Manager Taiyaba Khatoon

Publishing Assistant Halima Mohammed

Jacket Designer Jordan Lambley

Cartographer Ashif

Cartography Manager Suresh Kumar

Senior DTP Designer Tanveer Zaidi

Senior Production Editor Jason Little

Senior Production Controller Samantha Cross

Deputy Managing Editor Beverly Smart

Managing Editors Shikha Kulkarni, Hollie Teague

Managing Art Editor Sarah Snelling

Senior Managing Art Editor Priyanka Thakur

Art Director Maxine Pedliham

Publishing Director Georgina Dee

DK would like to thank the following for their contribution to the previous editions: Ron Emmons, Paul Gray, David Henley, Peter Holmshaw, Leena Lane, Helen Peters, Alex Robinson, Rough Guides / Martin Richardson

The publisher would like to thank the following for their kind permission to reproduce their photographs:
Key: a-above; b-below/bottom; c-centre; f-far; l-left; r-right; t-top

123RF.com: Pisanu Kusonsaratool 46–7, Wichit Sawatdee 73cla, Mr. Rapisan Swangphon 88br, Seksan Wasuwat 96clb.

Alamy Stock Photo: age fotostock / Dave Stamboulis 56tl; Paul Brown 57tr; Chronicle 38tr; Thomas Cockrem 86ca; third cross 11cra; Giulio Ercolani 96t; EyeEm Mobile GmbH / Wanwisa Hernandez 63c; Kevin Foy 61crb; Peter Horree 80clb; imageBROKER / Dirk Bleyer 20-1, / Mara Brandl 60tl; John Kellerman 63tl, 73crb, 88ca; Kevin Foy 79bl; Mike Lawrance 70tr; Pakorn Lopattananakul 105bl; William Manning 33c; mediacolor's 15tr; Christian Müller 103cra; Peter Adams Photography Ltd 41; Massimo Piacentino 4clb; Pictorial Press Ltd 39tr; Igor Prahin 43t; Prisma Bildagentur AG / Raga Jose Fuste 4b; Sergi Reboredo 58cb; Simon Reddy 62br; Suriya Desatit 50bl, Raquel Mogado 75cr, vasa 49cra; Mervyn Rees 27tl; robertharding / Luca Tettoni 17cla; 69cr; Leonid Serebrennikov 86b; Dave Stamboulis 74tl; Rick Strange 35bl; Nunnicha Supagrit 95crb; Fabrizio Troiani 22–3; Ian Watt 102tl; ZUMA Press; Inc. 65cl.

Anantara Bangkok Riverside Resort & Spa: 90clb.

Baan Khanitha: 99cra.

Bangkok Marriott Hotel Sukhumvit: 100cl.

Banyan Tree Bangkok: 92bl.

Bridgeman Images: Luca Tettoni 6tr, 16c.

Calypso Cabaret: Dorling Kindersley / Alex Robinson 55bl, 101t.

Depositphotos Inc: tampatra@hotmail.com 14-5c.

Doll Museum, Bangkok: Dorling Kindersley / Alex Robinson 51cla.

Dreamstime.com: Aaa187 35cra; Ammcranfield 22cr; Assoonas 4cl; Atosan 7tr; Nontawat Boonmun 59tr; Carloscastilla 51tr; Kanjanee Chaisin 46tl; Jaromír Chalabala 3tr, 106-7; Chaopavit 13tl; Sakkarin Chinsoi 43br; Chirawan 10tl; Pitchathorn Chintakanon 40cla; Cowardlion 7br, 21tr, 31tl; Daagron 4cla; Ionut David 26cla; Oleg Doroshenko 41br; Finallast 41tl; Santiago Rodríguez Fontoba 12bl; Gnomeandi 11bc; Gow927 50t; Simon Hack 4cr; Jorg Hackemann 2tr, 18bc, 36–7, 87tr; Nasrul Hudayah 54t; Ifocus 62cla; Iphotothailand 2tl, 8-9; Lukasz Janyst 32cla; Boonchoo Kaewyai 72bl; Khellon 80ca; Olga Khoroshunova 32crb; Teerasak Khunrach 49b; Hathaichanok Losunthonchai 21cr; Mai9111 22clb; Aliaksandr Mazurkevich 22-3; Mhoohao 71cl; Pranodh Mongkolthavorn 3tl, 66-7; Moori 10ca; Luciano Mortula 77tr; Nalidsa Sukprasert 49tl; Chatchawan Narakornpijit 32-3; Nicousnake 18cla, 34bl; Ongchangwei 11cb; Outcast85 104-5; Sean Pavone 4crb; Anton Petrus 6cl; Dmitry Pichugin 103b; Apichat Pimsoda 33tc; Thanapat Pirmphol 60b; Pixattitude 30c; Pixs4u 21br; Presse750 47tr; Sakol Promla 32-3; Psstockfoto 96-7; RIRFStock 19tl; Saiko3p 14br, 22cla, 23cla, 32cra; Melissa Schalke 11tl; Lee Snider 33tl; Nataliia Sokolovska 20bl; Maposee Soleh 34tr; Chatchai Somwat 47cl; Srckomkrit 10cb; StrippedPixel 76cl; Svglass 10br; Syda Productions 65tr; Tang90246 28cla; Tea 63br; Thaifairs 41cb; Tofudevil 19br; Tonfon 28br; Toxawww 27crb; Vladmax 85tr; Tawatchai Wanasri 42ca; Boaz Yunior Wibowo 69b; Wichits 12cl; Sirawut Wisutipaitoon 33crb; Noppasin Wongchum 10cl; Richard Van Der Woude 82-3; Minyun Zhou 26br.

Gaggan: 59bl.

Getty Images: AFP / Pornchai Kittiwongsakul 48clb; AWL / Gavin Hellier 89t; Paula Bronstein 39cl; Greg Elms 28-9; Kangheewan 70b; LightRocket / David Longstreath 64clb; Lonely Planet Images / Frank Carter 78t; Matteo Colombo / DigitalVision 1; Moment / Mongkol Chuewong 52-3; Moment / thebang 104clb; Seng Chye Teo, 94ca; Universal History Archive 38cb.

Grand Hyatt Erawan Bangkok: 45cr.

Hard Rock Café Bangkok: 93tl.

iStockphoto.com: aluxum 64t.

The Jim Thompson House: Dorling Kindersley / Alex Robinson 30cla, 30br, 31crb.

Maggie Choo's: 56b, 93cr.

Mandarin Oriental, Bangkok: 44tr, 55cr, 58t.

National Museum, Bangkok: Dorling Kindersley / Alex Robinson 17bl, 68tl.

Robert Harding Picture Library: Kay Maeritz 16cla; Marco Simoni 19bl; Luca Tettoni 11cr, 14cla, 84cla.

Shangri-La Hotel Bangkok: 44bl.

Shutterstock: Kayo 33br, Tooykrub 54bl.

The Sukhothai Bangkok: 99cb.

Tower Club at lebua: 91cra.

Cover images:
Front and spine: **Getty Images:** Matteo Colombo / DigitalVision.

Back: **AWL Images:** Jon Arnold tl; **Getty Images:** Matteo Colombo / DigitalVision b; **iStockphoto.com:** kitchakron crb, Yotsaran tr.

Pull out map cover image:
Getty Images: Matteo Colombo / DigitalVision.

Cartography: Jasneet Kaur, Zafar ul Islam Khan, Suresh Kumar, James Macdonald, Reetu Pandey.

All other images © Dorling Kindersley
For further information see:
www.dkimages.com

Penguin
Random
House

First edition in 2008

Published in Great Britain by
Dorling Kindersley Limited
DK, One Embassy Gardens, 8 Viaduct
Gardens, London SW11 7BW, UK

The authorised representative in the EEA is
Dorling Kindersley Verlag GmbH. Arnulfstr.
124, 80636 Munich, Germany

Published in the United States by
DK Publishing, 1745 Broadway, 20th Floor,
New York, NY 10019, USA

ISSN 1479-344X

ISBN 978-0-2415-6895-8

Printed and bound in Malaysia

www.dk.com

As a guide to abbreviations in visitor information blocks: **Adm** = admission charge; **D** = dinner **L** = lunch.

MIX
Paper | Supporting
responsible forestry
FSC™ C018179
www.fsc.org

This book was made with Forest
Stewardship Council™ certified
paper – one small step in DK's
commitment to a sustainable future.
**For more information go to
www.dk.com/our-green-pledge**

Phrase Book

Thai is a tonal language and regarded by most linguists as head of a distinct language group, though it incorporates many Sanskrit words from ancient India, and some of modern English ones, too. There are five tones: mid, high, low, rising, and falling. The particular tone, or pitch, at which each syllable is pronounced determines its meaning. For instance "mãi" (falling tone) means "not," but "mäi" (rising tone) is "silk." In the second column of this phrase book is a phonetic transliteration of the Thai script for English speakers, including guidance for tones in the form of accents. In polite speech, Thai men add **"krúp"** at the end of each sentence; women add **"kã"** at the end of questions and **"kä"** at the end of statements.

Guidelines for Pronunciation

When reading the phonetics, pronounce syllables as if they form English words. For instance:

a	as in "ago"
e	as in "hen"
i	as in "thin"
o	as in "on"
u	as in "gun"
ah	as in "rather"
ai	as in "Thai"
air	as in "pair"
ao	as in "Mao Zedong"
ay	as in "day"
er	as in "enter"
ew	as in "few"
oh	as in "go"
oo	as in "boot"
OO	as in "book"
oy	as in "toy"
g	as in "give"
ng	as in "sing"

These sounds have no close equivalents in English:

eu	can be likened to a sound of disgust - the sound could be written as "errgh"
bp	a single sound between a "b" and a "p"
dt	a single sound between a "d" and a "t"

Note that when "p," "t," and "k" occur at the end of Thai words, the sound is "swallowed." Also note that many Thais use an "l" instead of an "r" sound

The Five Tones

Accents indicate the tone of each syllable.

no mark	The **mid tone** is voiced at the speaker's normal, even pitch.
á é í ó ú	The **high tone** is pitched slightly higher than the mid tone.
à è ì ò ù	The **low tone** is pitched slightly lower than the mid tone.
ã ẽ ĩ õ ũ	The **rising tone** sounds like a questioning pitch, starting low and rising.
â ê î ô û	The falling tone sounds similar to an syllable word for emphasis.

In an Emergency

Help!	chôo-ay dôo-ay!
Fire!	fai mâi!
Where is the nearest hospital?	tãir-o-nêe mee rohng pa-yah-bahn yòo tēe-nài?
Call an ambulance!	rêe-uk rót pa-yah-bahn hâi nòy!
Call a doctor!	rêe-uk mŏr hâi nòy!
Call the police!	rêe-uk dtum ròo-ut hâi nòy!

Communication Essentials

Yes	châi or krúp/kâ
No	mâi châi or mâi krúp/mâi kâ
Please can you…?	chôo-ay
Thank you	kòrp-kOOn
No, thank you	mâi ao kòrp-kOOn
Excuse me/sorry	kŏr-tôht (krúp/kâ)
Hello	sa-wùt dee (krúp/kã)
Goodbye	lah gòrn ná
What?	a-rai?
Why?	tum-mai?
Where?	têe nài?
How?	yung ngai?

Useful Phrases

How are you?	kOOn sa-bai dee reu (krúp/kã)?
Very well, thank you	sa-bai dee (krúp/kã)
How do I get to…?	…bpai yung-ngai?
Do you speak English?	kOOn pôot pah-sãh ung-grìt bpen mái?
Could you speak slowly?	chôo-ay pôot chah-cháh nòy dâi mái?
I can't speak Thai.	pôot pah-sãh tai mâi bpen

Useful Words

hot	rórn
cold	yen or nǎo
good	dee
bad	mâi dee
enough	por
open	bpèrt
closed	bpìt
left	sái
right	kwãh
near	glâi
far	glai
straight ahead	yòo dtrong nâh
woman/women	pŏo-yĩng
man/men	pŏo-chai
child/children	dèk
entrance	tahng kào
exit	tahng òrk
toilet	hôrng nãhm

Keeping in Touch

Where is the nearest public telephone?	tãir-o nêe mee toh-ra-sùp yòo têe-nài?
Can I call abroad from here?	ja toh bpai dtàhng bpra-tâyt jàhk têe nêe dâi mái?
Hello, this is… speaking.	hello (pŏm /dee-chún)…pôot (krúp/kâ)
May I leave a message?	kŏr fâhk sùng a-rai nòy dâi mái?
I would like to speak to…	kŏr pôot gùp khun… nòy (krúp/kã)
local call	toh-ra-sùp pai nai tórng tìn
phone card	but toh-ra-sùp

Shopping

How much does this cost?	nêe rah-kah tâo-rài?
I would like…	dtôrng-gahn…
Do you have?	mee… mái?
I am just looking	chom doo tâo-nún
Do you take credit cards/travelers' checks?	rub but cray-dìt/ chék dern tang mái?
What time do you open/close?	bpèrt/bpìt gèe mohng?
Can you ship this overseas?	sóng khõng nee bpai dtàhng bpra-tâyt dâi mái?
Could you lower the price a bit?	lót rah-kah nòy dâi mái?
How about…baht?	…bàht dâi mái?
That's a little expensive.	pairng bpai nòy
Will you go for… baht?	…bàht bpai mái?
I'll settle for… baht.	…bàht gôr láir-o-gun
cheap	tòok
expensive	pairng
Does it come in other colors?	mee sẽe èun èek mái?
black	sẽe dum
blue	sẽe núm ngern
green	sẽe kẽe-o
red	sẽe dairng
white	sẽe kão
yellow	sẽe lẽu-ung
gold	torng
silver	ngern
Thai silk	pâh-mãi tai
ladies' wear	sèu-pâh sa-dtree
bookstore	ráhn kãi núng-sẽu
department store	hâhng
pharmacy	ráhn kãi yah
market	dta-làht
newsstand	ráhn kãi núng-sẽu pim
shoe shop	ráhn kãi rorng táo
supermarket	sŌOp-bpèr-mah-gèt
tailor	ráhn dtùt sêu-a

Staying in a Hotel

Do you have a vacant room?	mee hôrng wâhng mái?
air-conditioned room	hôrng air
I have a reservation.	jorng hôrng wái láir-o
I'd like a room for one night/three nights.	(pôm/dee-chún) ja púk yòo keun nèung/ sãhm keun
What is the charge per night?	kâh hôrng wun la tâo-rái?
I don't know yet how long I'll stay	mâi sâhp wâh ja yòo nahn tâo-rài
May I see the room first please?	kõr doo hôrng gòrn dâi mái?
May I leave some things in the safe?	kõr fâhk kõrng wái nai dtôo sáyf dâi mái?
Will you spray some mosquito repellent, please?	chôo-ay chèet yah gun yŌOng hâi nòy dâi mái?
double/twin room	hôrng kôo
single room	hôrng dèe-o
bedroom	hôrng norn
bill	bin
fan	pùt lom

Sightseeing

hotel	rohng-rairm
key	gOOn-jair
manager	pôo-jùt-gahn
mosquito screen	mŌOng lôo-ut
shower	fùk boo-a
swimming pool	sá wâi náhm
travel agent	bor-rí sùt num têe-o
tourist office	sũm-núk ngahn gahn tôrng têe-o
tourist police	dtum-ròo-ut tôrng têe-o
beach	háht or chai-háht
cliff	nâh pãh
festival	ngahn órk rãhn
hill/mountain	kão
historical park	ÒO-ta-yahn-bpra wùt sàht
island (koh)	gòr
lake	ta-lay sáhp
museum	pí-pít-ta-pun
national park	ÒO-ta yahn háirng châht
palace	wang
park/garden	sõo-un
river	mâir náhm
ruins	boh-rahn sa-tãhn
temple (wat)	wút
Thai boxing	moo-ay tai
Thai massage	nôo-ut
trekking	gahn dern tahng táo
waterfall	náhm dtòk
zoo	sõo-un sàt

Transportation

When does the train for…leave?	rót fai bpai…òrk meu-rài?
How long does it take to get to…?	chái way-lah nahn tâo-rài bpai tẽung têe…?
A ticket to… please.	kõr dtõ-a bpai… nòy (krúp/kâ)
Which platform for the… train?	rót fai bpai… yòo chahn cha-lah nãi?
What station is this?	têe nêe sa-tãhn-nee a-rai?
I'd like to reserve a seat, please.	kõr jorng têe nùng
Where is the bus station?	sa-tãhn-nee rót may yòo têe-nãi?
Which buses go to…?	rót may sãi nãi bpai…?
What times does the bus for… leave?	rót may bpai… òrk gèe mohng?
Would you tell me when we get to… ?	tẽung… láir-o chôo-ay bòrk dôo-ay?
Is it far?	glai mái?
ticket	dtõo-a
air-conditioned bus	rót bprùp ah-gàht
airport	sa-nãhm bin
tour bus	rót too-a
train	rót fai
bus station	sa-tãhn-nee rót may
moped	rót mor-dter-sai
bicycle	rót jùk-gra-yahn
taxi	táirk-sêe

Eating Out

A table for two please.	kõr dtó sũm-rùp sõrng kon

May I see the menu?	kŏr doo may-noo nòy?
Do you have… ?	mee… mái?
I'd like…	kŏr…
I didn't order this.	nêe mâi dâi sùng (krûp/kâ)
Is it spicy?	mâi ao pèt
Not too spicy, ok?	pèt mái? máhk na
I can eat Thai food.	tahn ah-hăhn tai bpen
May I have a glass of water, please.	kŏr núm kâirng bplào gâir-o nèung
Waiter/waitress!	kOOn (krúp/kâ)
The check, please.	kŏr bin nòy (krúp/kâ)
bottle	kòo-ut
chopsticks	dta-gée-up
drink(s)	krêu-ung dèum
fork	sôm
glass	gâir-o
menu	may-noo
spoon	chórn

Menu Decoder

nòr mái	bamboo shoots
glôoy-ay	banana
néu-a woo-a	beef
bee-a	beer
dtôm	boiled
yâhng	char-grilled
gài	chicken
prík	chili
gah-fair	coffee
bpoo	crab
mèe gròrp	crispy noodles
gŏo-ay dtĕe-o hâirng	dry noodles
bpèt	duck
tOO-ree-un	durian
kài	egg
bplah	fish
king	ginger
núm kâirng bplào	iced water
ka-nÕOn	jackfruit
mâir-kŏhng	Mekong Whisky
hèt	mushroom
gŏo-ay dtĕe-o-náhm	noodle soup
ma-la-gor	papaya
sùp-bpa-rót	pineapple
néu-a-mŏo	pork
kâo	rice
gŏo-ay dtĕe-o	rice noodles
gÔOng	shrimp
núm see éw	soup
ah-hăhn wâhng	soy sauce
pùk ka-náh	spring greens
kâo-nĕe-o	sticky rice
kâo pòht	sweet corn
núm chah	tea
pùk	vegetables
náhm	water

Health

I do not feel well	róá-sèuk mâi sa-bai
It hurts here.	jèp dtrong née
I have a fever.	dtoo-a-rórn bpen kâi
sore throat	jèp kor
stomach ache	bpòo-ut tórng
vomit	ah-jee-un
asthma	rôhk hèut
cough	ai
diabetes	róhk bao wăhn
diarrhea	tórng sĕe-a
dizzy	wee-un hŏo-a
dysentry	rôhk bìt
fever	kâi
headache	bpòo-ut hŏo-a
aspirin	air-sa-bprin or yah-gâir kâi
doctor	mŏr
dentist	tun-dta-pàirt or mŏr fun
hospital	rohng pa-yah-bahn
injection	chèet yah
medicine	yah
prescription	bai sùng yah
How many tablets do I take?	dtôrng gin yah gèe mét dtòr krúng
I'm allergic to…	(pŏm/dee-chún) páir…

Numbers

0	sŏon
1	nèung
2	sŏrng
3	săhm
4	sèe
5	hâh
6	hòk
7	jèt
8	bpàirt
9	gâo
10	sìp
11	sìp-èt
12	sìp-sŏrng
13	sìp-săhm
14	sìp-sèe
15	sìp-hâh
16	sìp-hòk
17	sìp-jét
18	sìp-bpàirt
19	sìp-gâo
20	yêe-sìp
30	săhm-sìp
40	sèe-sìp
50	hâh-sìp
60	hòk-sìp
70	jèt-sìp
80	bpàirt-sìp
90	gâo-sìp
100	nèung róy
1,000	nèung pun
10,000	nèung mèun
100,000	nèung săirn

Time

one minute	nèung nah-tee
one hour	nèung chôo-a mohng
half an hour	krêung chôo-a mohng
Sunday	wun ah-tít
Monday	wun jun
Tuesday	wun ung-kahn
Wednesday	wun pÖOt
Thursday	wun pa-réu-hùt
Friday	wun sÖOk
Saturday	wun săo
a day	neung wun
a week	nèung ah-tít
a weekend	sÕOt súp-pah-dah
a month	nèung deu-un
a year	nèung bpee